a POCKET ESSENTIAL

SHORT INTRODUCTION
TO
RELIGION

Also by Gordon Kerr

a POCKET ESSENTIAL

SHORT INTRODUCTION
TO
RELIGION

GORDON KERR

Oldcastle Books

First published in 2019
by Oldcastle Books Ltd,
PO Box 394, Harpenden, Herts, AL5 1XJ
www.pocketessentials.com

Editor: Nick Rennison

A CIP catalogue record for this book is available from the British Library.

ISBN
978-0-85730-170-3 (print)
978-0-85730-171-0 (epub)

Typeset by Avocet Typeset, Somerton, Somerset, TA11 6RT
in 12pt Adobe Garamond Pro
Printed and bound in Great Britain by Clays Elcograf S.p.A.

In memory of Hazel Baker

'Just as a candle cannot burn without fire,
men cannot live without a spiritual life'
Buddha

CONTENTS

Introduction 11

Prehistory 15

Religions of Antiquity 23
  1: Ancient Egypt 24
  2: Zoroastrianism 30
  3: Ancient Greece 39
  4: Ancient Rome 48
  5: Celtic Religions 53
  6: Norse Religions 58
  7: Religions of the Nomads 62
  8: Pre-Colombian American Religions 68

Religions of India 79
  9: Hinduism 80
  10: Buddhism 101
  11: Jainism 119
  12: Sikhism 127

Religions of the East 137
  13: China 138
  14: Japan 147

CONTENTS

Abrahamic Religions   157
15: Judaism   158
16: Christianity   176
17: Islam   204

Independent Belief Systems   219

New Religious Movements   233

Bibliography   248

Index   249

Introduction

What is religion? At first, this appears to be a question with an easy answer. It is the worship of a divine being or beings in order to receive something in return, whether it be a good harvest, long life, healthy children, spiritual happiness, entry to heaven, the freedom from fear, or any of the myriad other things that people seek when they create a system of belief. It is not quite that simple, of course, because religion works for believers on many levels. It certainly encompasses spiritual elements, and has important personal aspects, but it also takes on social and political ones too. It is deeply engrained in our lives, even if we are not believers, because not believing also implies a deal of thought about how our lives are guided, why we are here and how we have come to exist. One thing is certain, however – the phenomenon of religion, of trying to explain the world to ourselves and our communities and to extract some benefit from the spiritual, has been an ever-present part of our existence from time immemorial. It can be found in every culture from prehistoric times to the twenty-first century. We see it from the cave paintings and burial behaviour of our ancestors right up to some of the bizarre new religions of today.

Religion has always provided believers with a means of understanding the world around them, but also of being able to ensure that powerful natural phenomena work in a community's favour. The weather, the seasons and the fundamental events of life, such as birth, death, war and illness, were all explained away in religious terms and were often allocated deities for whom one or several of these events and phenomena was a responsibility. They lived in often fantastic realms that were beyond the one in which human beings live. Religion provided the context within which such inaccessible beings could be communicated with in order to seek their help with the problems of everyday life. Prayer has often been the method used and ritual is employed to evoke these spirits or to please them and demonstrate that we care for them. This can be clearly seen in the Japanese religion of Shinto where the spirits known as *kami* are engaged in a mutually beneficial relationship with people, one with benefits for each side. In other words, keep the *kami* happy and they will see that you have what you want for a fulfilled life. Of course, such worship is often done in a communal setting, thus welding together a particular society in a shared faith and giving it a collective identity that helps it survive in challenging times and encourages its members to work hard for each other. It is also, of course, a means by which the elite can keep the people beneath them in the hierarchy under their control.

Religion has survived persecution, war, suppression and the constraints that society has placed upon it because faith, by its very nature, is nothing if not resilient. And even in our materialistic world, where so much of what people used to invest with religious belief is now explained by science, religion persists. In fact, roughly three-quarters of the world's population consider themselves to hold some sort of religious conviction, whether it be faith in God, or the conviction that alien beings are going to arrive on earth and somehow make everything alright. So, it can safely be said that we need religion, that it is an essential part of living on our planet.

It is estimated that there are around 4,200 religions in the world. These range from the major religions, such as Christianity and Islam, whose adherents number many millions, down to indigenous faith systems that are practised by the inhabitants of just one village or community. Over the millennia other religions, with their own distinct beliefs, rituals and mythology, have come and gone, or been assimilated by another larger faith or, as has often been the case, by the religion of a conquering or occupying power. Probably the oldest surviving of all these religions is Hinduism which grew out of the folk religions of India and first emerged in the compiling of the Vedas almost two and a half millennia ago. The magnificent Vedic tradition also contributed to the later emergence of Jainism, Buddhism and Sikhism. The Far East saw the rise of its own religious traditions, traditional folk religions blending into Daoism and Confucianism. Meanwhile, the ancient powers of Greece and Rome developed their own idiosyncratic religions with their pantheons of gods. East of the Mediterranean world, Zoroastrianism – to our knowledge, the world's first major monotheistic faith – was established in Persia and Judaism, the earliest of the Abrahamic traditions, emerged, to be followed by Christianity and Islam. Religions continue to adapt to the challenges of the modern world and still newer ones have emerged, in all religious traditions, sometimes incorporating elements of what has gone before.

It would, of course, be impossible to cover every religion.

However, in these pages, you will learn some of the fascinating histories of the world's better-known faith systems as well as accounts of the lives of the men who founded them and sometimes gave everything for them. Sacred texts, beliefs, rituals and practices are also detailed.

At a time when cultures and civilisations are clashing in various parts of the modern world, it helps to gain an understanding of the faith that drives people to do incredible or sometimes evil things. *A Pocket Essential Introduction to Religion* provides a very good starting point for further study.

Prehistory

Prehistoric Speculation

Religious awareness probably developed around the time that humankind first emerged on Earth – around two or three million years ago – but, in the absence of evidence, this is difficult to prove. Various finds have suggested some kind of religious consciousness, such as burial places; the placing of offerings; carved idols; reliefs and paintings on rocks and in caves, possibly representing deities, spirits and cultic figures; and structures such as altars, temples and pillars that possibly have religious associations. But all of this can be little more than speculation.

If religious thinking did exist, its beliefs and mythology would have been transmitted orally as well as through ritual, but it is possible that many people would have been too preoccupied with just surviving to have much to do with religious belief. What beliefs did exist would have been a good deal more simplistic in pre-literate than in literate times and pre-literate religion would almost certainly have focused on the activities of people at the time – fishing, hunting, gathering food or early types of agriculture. They would be practised in limited tribal societies in which family groupings or kin-groups were hugely important and nature would have had a great deal of influence, just as it did on prehistoric people's daily lives.

During the Paleolithic period – the Old Stone Age – people were hunters, food-gatherers or fishermen. By the Neolithic – the New Stone Age – hunters had, on the whole, become farmers and pastoral nomadism developed from this. Two and a half million years ago, early humankind was using tools such as choppers, scrapers and other stone implements they had made themselves. Work was divided between the sexes and food was shared. But still we do not know what their religious convictions were, or if, indeed, they possessed any.

One of the early representatives of *Homo erectus* was Peking Man, a group of fossil specimens found during excavations at Zhoukoudian near modern-day Beijing between 1923 and 1927. The skulls that were discovered were broken at the *foramen magnum*, one of the openings at the base of the skull. This allowed access to the brain which, it is presumed, was removed and eaten for what were probably ritual, magical or religious purposes. In today's primitive societies, such behaviour is practised so that the consumer of the material somehow assumes the energy or strength of the person being consumed and one might presume this was the case back then. Again, however, all of this is mere speculation.

It is with Neanderthal Man that more concrete evidence of religious practices comes to light. Neanderthals, a sub-species of the genus *Homo*, became extinct around 40,000 years ago. They carried out ceremonies in which they buried their dead and it would appear that they believed in life after death. In one instance, in a cave at Monte Circeo in Italy, a Neanderthal skull was discovered surrounded by a circle of stones and 'skull burials' were common throughout the Paleolithic period. What appear to be sacred objects have also been found, items such as round fossils and iron pyrites.

Neanderthal people were replaced by a new species, our ancestor, *Homo sapiens*, and by the end of the Lower Paleolithic period, around 300,000 years ago, they had already spread across the world. Probably around 60,000 years ago, Siberian peoples first crossed into the Americas. More than 30,000 years ago Australia was peopled by humans from Indonesia. These movements suggest that the hunting religions that developed in Australia and America, in all likelihood date back to those times.

It is in the Upper Paleolithic period – roughly between 50,000 and 10,000 years ago – that we see greater examples of religious belief. Burials by hunting people in that era make it clear that they believed in life after death. In southeast France skeletons have been found that are stained with iron oxide and adorned with bracelets. They are even furnished with flint knives and quartzite tools. Property that was special to the dead was buried with them so that they would have use of it in the next life. This can be seen at burial sites from Italy to Russia.

Prehistoric Religious Art

The famous 'Venus' figurines date from around that time. These idols, the most famous of which is the 'Venus of Willendorf', found by a worker in Willendorf in Austria in 1908, are sculpted from ivory, stone and bone and have been found from France to eastern Siberia. The bodies of the figures are distorted, especially those parts associated with fertility and child-bearing. Some have suggested that they are no more than representations of women of the time. It seems likely, however, from the focus on fertility and sexual functions, that these figures are representations of deities of fertility and fruitfulness. It is, of course, odd that female gods should be so prominent in a society that was based on hunting, undertaken by men. But female birth deities were common, for example in north Eurasian cultures, providing protection during pregnancy and childbirth. Siberian peoples believed in a mother of the animals whom she brought into being and protected.

Cave paintings are probably the best-known remnant of prehistoric art. Appearing in the Upper Paleolithic period, from about 15,000 BC to 11,000 BC, they are most commonly found in southern France and the north of Spain. 80 per cent of these illustrations are of animals, mainly horses and bison, although reindeer began to be represented late in the period, as the glaciers moved southwards. Could they have been executed in order to secure a bountiful hunt? The representation of an animal might have been a means of ensuring that such a creature was killed in the hunt. We are unsure why the paintings and engravings were done in caves. It was possibly a result of the belief that animals came from under the ground, or once, perhaps, lived in the caves. Scenes showing human figures clothed in animal skins may depict ritualistic performers or even mythical beings.

It is, as ever, difficult to be certain and many images do not really support the assumptions above but it does seem as if, in the Upper Paleolithic period in Europe, there could have been a type of religion or magical belief centred around fertility and animals. There are examples of reindeer skeletons buried in Siberia, the hope being that the animal would be restored to life either in this world or in another life after death.

Religion in Neolithic Times

The Neolithic period – roughly from 10,000 to 3,000 BC – brought the birth of agriculture which allowed the rapidly increasing population of the world – numbering at the time probably around 10 million – to create settlements. Villages were established, and crafts such as pottery developed. In the west Mediterranean, cemeteries have been found on the outskirts of villages whose graves contain gifts and offerings, including female figurines, perhaps intended as servants or to provide comfort in the afterlife. They may even have symbolised goddesses, there to provide protection. Through time, these graves began to vary, according to social status, as some members of the society benefited from the production of surplus products that stability brought and achieved not just wealth but also rank. Bodies began to be buried and coffins began to be used. Eventually cremation was occasionally practised, speaking of a more sophisticated or even more spiritual perception of the afterlife.

The discovery of full-figured female figurines carved from terracotta, bone or clay, suggests that fertility cults existed. They also emphasise the more prominent position of women in this new agrarian society where they had an important role to play. The mother goddess's functions were also reflected in this change. She was now a goddess of earth and vegetation. There were many other types of fertility goddesses, and snakes were often to be found wrapped around the figure's body. In many parts of the world, the snake was at the time a fertility symbol.

Large buildings for the purpose of worship began to replace

the random places selected by the people of the earlier nomadic hunting culture. Sacred, ritualistic objects such as altars, vases emblazoned with ritualistic imagery and sculptures and temples have been found, for instance, in Ukraine and the surrounding region.

Eastern Asia mirrors developments in the Neolithic period in Europe and Western Asia, but Southeast Asia is more complex and it is more difficult to be precise. Meanwhile, in America, agrarian rituals seem to have not been very different to those of the hunters. The Neolithic period prevailed in certain areas of agricultural America until Columbus arrived in 1492 and even after that.

Monuments

It is thought that most of the monuments made up of large stones – megaliths – that began to appear towards the end of the Neolithic Age were for the purpose of burial. These dolmens – single-chamber megalithic tombs – consisted of large flat stones that were supported on large upright stones.

But, as can be found at Carnac in Brittany, there were also sites where massive stones were placed in alignment. We are ignorant of their purpose, but one theory suggests that they signified ritual procession routes. At Tarxien in southeastern Malta, the Hal Tarxien stone structures seem to have been temples and inside have been found sculptures carved out of chalk that depict human features and gowns. These may be representative of priests and/or the gods and goddesses they worshipped.

Of course, there are other megalithic structures that

appear to possess merely an astronomical function, guiding agriculturalists on when to plant their seeds, for instance. The circle of sarsen stones at Stonehenge on Salisbury Plain in England lines up with the sunrise at midsummer but Stonehenge also seems to have been a place of worship. This type of structure has been found around the world, described by astronomers and experts on prehistory as observatories and megalithic calendars. Nonetheless, this type of astronomy was almost certainly undertaken within a religious context. Soon, around 3,000 BC, great civilisations would be emerging in the river plains in Egypt and Mesopotamia as well as in other areas of the Middle East and Western Asia. The religion that developed there would be distinguished by sacred kings, a religious hierarchy of priests, ritual sacrifice and grand temples. Gods and goddesses would be the subjects of veneration and the afterlife would be delineated.

Religions of Antiquity

1

Ancient Egypt

'Man, know thyself, and you are going to know the Gods.'
Inscription from Luxor Temple, Egypt

The Religion of Ancient Egypt

The fabulous Ancient Egyptian civilisation existed in the lower reaches of the Nile Valley from about 3100 BC until 30 BC, when it became a province of the Roman Empire under Octavian, the future Emperor Augustus (r. 27 BC-14 AD). It is defined by several important periods – the Old Kingdom (c. 2700-2200 BC), the time of powerful pharaohs who left a legacy of mighty pyramids; the Middle Kingdom (c. 2000-1800 BC), also dubbed the Period of Reunification; and the New Kingdom (c. 1550-1225 BC), a time when Egypt was a pre-eminent power in the region. At other times, outside these periods of strength, Egypt was plagued with internal fighting, weak rulers or suffered foreign occupation. During these times, religious customs and beliefs changed, but because there are so many consistencies, it is still possible to discuss what can be termed 'the religion of Egypt'.

Early Egyptian religion can only be explained by referring to objects that have been found before writing first appeared in around 3100 BC. These objects – items such as amulets – are concerned most often with hunting or fertility. There are earthenware figurines of naked women which undoubtedly were about fertility and the aspiration to have many children. Elephant tusk pendants that have been found were probably worn to provide protection for the hunter and guarantee him a successful hunt. Religious rituals are hinted at in pictures painted on pots or scratched on rocks but it is impossible to say precisely what they mean.

Egyptian gods are a bizarre collection of half-animal, half-human entities, many of them representing elements of the natural world. It is understandable that Egyptians should embrace the natural world for its deities as the country depended on natural phenomena for survival, and the annual flooding of the River Nile was vitally important. It was this that made the land fertile and enabled Egyptian farmers to grow crops. Such important gods needed to be placated with worship and sacrifice and they were often depicted as animals or birds. The sun god, for instance, was represented by a hawk and the cobra, symbolized Renenutet, the goddess of the harvest.

Cities, too, had deities associated with them. When Thebes was the capital of Egypt during the New Kingdom, for instance, its god, Amun, became a deity who protected the entire nation. But local gods were worshipped in other towns and people would also worship deities that were important to them, such as ones relevant to their profession. A writer, might, for example, worship Thoth, the deity associated with scribes. The pharaoh could himself be a god and so could outstanding individuals.

There is also believed to have been a single deity who is unnamed but who controlled the universe and maintained the balance between good and evil. In fact, in the 25 years between 1375 BC and 1350 BC, the pharaoh Amenhotep IV (r. 1353-1336 BC or 1351-1334 BC), a man whose sanity has sometimes been questioned, although others have described him as a visionary, promoted the worship of one god, Aten – the sun's disc. During his reign, worship of other gods was forbidden. Aten came to be regarded as the source of all life and this power was passed to the king who changed his name to Akhenaten (translated as 'the one who is beneficial to the Aten'). Whether this move was religious or political, we do not know. Amenhotep may simply have been trying to bring some unity and stability to a nation in turmoil. Whatever the reason, the reform was not well received and the status quo was restored shortly after his death.

Animals were often deified. Sometimes it would be an entire species and great numbers of baboons, crocodiles, ibises and cats and dogs were mummified and buried. But an individual animal could also be deified. The creature would lead a wonderful life before being mummified and ritually buried on its death.

Daily Worship in Ancient Egypt

Gods were treated like humans in Ancient Egyptian ritual. They were wakened in the morning with a choir as part of a morning ritual, and the god's night clothing was removed from its image. It was then washed, dressed, fed and given something to drink – the food and drink taking the form of offerings. The day continued with the god – or, rather, the image of the god – receiving visitors, being involved in prophesies or other duties. These, of course, were interpreted and delivered by priests which gave these men a considerable amount of power and influence. Offerings of sustenance would be made to the god during the day and he would be put to bed in his shrine at night. These images have not survived but we surmise they were made of stone or precious metal, and, one presumes, given the level of worship, would have been adorned with elaborate ornamentation.

Festivals were also part of the life of a god and his worshippers, some consisting of a mere offering or a ritual or procession in the temple. Others involved lengthy voyages on the Nile, perhaps to visit another god's temple. These longer festivals were holidays for the Egyptians. As the god's shrine floated past on his barge, worshippers, who sometimes travelled considerable distances to be there, would line the river banks, cheering. One document estimates a crowd of around 700,000 pilgrims gathered for one festival. The ornate shrine could not be seen by worshippers as it was carried by a number of bearers on a boat-shaped platform. In the river festivals, the shrine would travel on a vessel made of wood, specially constructed to look very much like the reed boats from the periods when such festivals probably originated.

After originating in duties performed by local dignitaries, the priesthood evolved into a professional body and occasionally, when a weak pharaoh occupied the throne, the high priest of one of the main Egyptian gods was de facto ruler. There was a hierarchy of religious officials, and women could serve as priestesses.

Mythology, Stories and The Book of the Dead

There was no main holy book in Egyptian religion and very few stories of the gods have survived. Some fragments have been assembled into what might be complete stories but we have no way of knowing if these are correct. The Ancient Egyptians appear to have believed the universe was originally filled with water from which a hill emerged that supported life. This, of course, relates to their own existence and the annual subsiding of the life-giving Nile flood waters. The gods emerged from this hill, they believed, and created other gods. Prayers and hymns were written and there were books of wisdom, the contents of which ranged from everyday advice to moral principles and ponderings on the nature of life. They contained guidance, too, on how to live a pious life and, thereby, to please the gods as well as gain the good opinion of other people, thus guaranteeing safe passage to the afterlife. Many images of the time depict the heart of a deceased person being weighed against a feather, the result of which was recorded by the scribe of the gods, Thoth. Osiris was always shown to be present at this ceremony. To be found wanting at this stage meant eternal destruction.

The afterworld was important to Ancient Egyptians, as is evident from the food and other items left in tombs from an early date. Later, the images used to decorate tomb walls depict how the Egyptians perceived the afterlife. It reflected this world but in it everything was much better, with bountiful harvests, pretty girls and sumptuous banquets. It did evolve, however. The king was originally believed to spend his time after death with the sun god Ra as he travelled across the sky on his daily journey, but, later, deceased kings began to be associated with Osiris who became the god of the afterlife, the underworld and the dead. As time passed, the association with Osiris spread to include not just the king but all classes of people.

The journey to the afterworld was an arduous and dangerous one, and the spirit of the deceased encountered all kinds of obstacles and demons en route. Reciting incantations from a roll of papyrus defeated these enemies, allowing the dead person to pass unhindered. These books, or rolls of papyrus are sometimes called *The Book of the Dead* although other names exist. Copies were deposited in the tomb for the use of the dead person and sometimes the incantations were inscribed inside the coffin or on the walls of the tomb itself.

Mummification was practised because the Ancient Egyptians believed that the spirit still needed the physical body after death. In cases where the body was not available, if the person had been lost at sea or perished in a fire, for instance, a statue of the dead person or even a painting would be sufficient. The funeral ceremony itself consisted of a ritual named 'The Opening of the Mouth'. The mouth and other bodily orifices were treated in such a way that they remained open so that the deceased might be able to eat as well as see and hear and perform other bodily functions after death.

2

Zoroastrianism

'Truth is best (of all that is) good. As desired,
what is being desired is truth for him who
(represents) the best truth.'
Zoroaster, *Gathas* 27.14

Zoroaster

Zoroastrians follow the teachings of the Iranian prophet Zoroaster who is also known as Zarathustra. He most likely lived in the second millennium BC, although some scholars place him a little later, in the seventh and sixth centuries BC, perhaps around the time of Cyrus the Great (r. 559-530 BC) and Darius I (r. 522-486 BC), emperors of the Achaemenid Empire. His birthplace is unknown but he is said to have started training for the priesthood at the age of seven, graduating at fifteen. Aged twenty, he left home and travelled, but ten years later, at a spring festival, he experienced a revelation, in the form of a shining being on a riverbank. The being announced himself to be Vohu Manah (Good Purpose,

Good Mind or Good Thought). He taught Zoroaster about Ahura Mazda (Good Spirit) and five other radiant figures and Zoroaster became aware of two primal Spirits. The second of these was Angra Mainyu (Hostile Spirit) which had two opposing concepts – Asha (Truth, or Righteousness) and Druj (lie). More revelations followed, including a vision of the seven Amesha Spenta – divine entities. His teachings were collected in the Gathas and the Avesta.

Zoroaster was vehemently opposed to the oppressive class system in Persia which put him at odds with the authorities. His teachings, therefore, were initially rejected and he was forced to leave his home. According to those who believe in the later date for Zoroaster's life, when he was 42 years old, he found a patron, in Queen Hutaosa (550-475 BC) and a ruler, Vishtaspa (dates unknown, although he is presumed to be an historical figure), who had adopted Zoroaster's teachings at an early date. Zoroastrianism became the official religion of his small kingdom in northeast Persia, although its exact location is not known.

Zoroaster lived for many more years, establishing a faithful following. He married three times, had three sons and three daughters and died at the age of seventy-seven. Stories about his death vary, one saying that he died in a conflict with the Turan people of Persia, another suggesting that he was murdered by Bradres, a priest of the old religion. Following his death, his religion spread throughout Persia, eventually becoming the Persian Empire's officially sanctioned religion.

The Teaching of Zoroaster

Believers in Zoroastrianism consider their prophet to have been chosen by God to receive his unique revelation which is to be found in the Gathas, a collection of 17 hymns. The hymn form was chosen to transmit these ideas because it made it easier to commit the words to memory at a time when writing was not known and these hymns now form part of the *Yasna*, the principal act of worship in Zoroastrianism.

What distinguishes Zoroaster's teaching from others is his belief in the importance of personal religion, a notion that probably derives from the fact that God appeared to him personally. It is a personal responsibility, he teaches, for men and women to choose between good and evil and they will be judged after death on how well they chose during their life. If the good thoughts outweigh the evil in their lives, they will go to heaven, but those whose life shows greater evil than goodness will be sent to hell. Social status, wealth or position will have no bearing on their fate.

The sacred chord or girdle – the *kushti* – a symbol of priesthood to the Indo-Iranians, and a sacred, vest-like shirt made of white cotton, called a *sedreh*, formed the sacred armour that Zoroaster said would remind believers of their daily battle against evil. It is their ritual dress. The *kushti* is wound three times around the waist and tied twice in a double knot at the front and back. Its 72 fine, white, woollen threads represent the 72 chapters of the *Yasna*. The ritual of tying and untying the *kushti* – *Nirang-i Kushti* – is performed several times a day and during this ritual, the worshipper must stand in one spot and remain silent. The *sedreh* is an undergarment worn by Zoroastrians to protect them from evil. It has a small pocket at the front in which the wearer may collect his or her good deeds.

To Zoroaster, God – Ahura Mazda – was the creator of everything, described as a friend to all. The evil in the world emanated from the Destructive Spirit, Angra Mainyu, creator of the demons, the ruler of hell and the enemy of God from the beginning of time. It is worth noting that, unlike in Christianity, Angra Mainyu, the equivalent of the Devil, is not a fallen angel because that would have made God responsible for him and, consequently, for evil, an unthinkable notion to Zoroastrians.

The Good Creator also created some heavenly beings. The Bounteous Immortals (Amesha Spentas), the sons and daughters of God, are the leading figures. They could be said to be the equivalent of the archangels found in a number of religious traditions. Rather than having human forms, they are fairly abstract, their names being Vohu Manah (Good Mind); Asha (Truth, or Righteousness); Armaiti (Devotion); Kshathra (Dominion); Haurvatat (Wholeness); and Ameretat (Immortality). These are heavenly beings, therefore, but also aspirations to which followers should devote themselves. There are seven creations of God that the Bounteous Immortals have to protect and which represent them. These are humanity, sky, waters, earth, plants, animals and fire. A representative of each of these, and by extension, of the Bounteous Immortal, is present at significant ceremonies or acts of worship, meaning that there is a symbolic representation of both the heavenly and the earthly worlds at all such events.

The world, Zoroaster taught, was basically good, although under constant attack from evil, but he foresaw the day when good will finally triumph, and the world will be restored to a state of perfection, the way the Good Creator had made it. At that point, the dead will rise and be judged. Those who have committed evil acts will be consigned to hell and the righteous will dwell in perfection with God throughout eternity.

The Story of Zoroastrianism

To the east of Europe, sometime round 3000 BC, a confederation of Indo-European tribes began to break up and go their separate ways. Some ventured south and established settlements in Greece and Rome, while others travelled north to Scandinavia. One group moved east to Persia (today's Iran) and some ventured as far as India. Those who ended up in Persia and India are most relevant to Zoroastrianism. Known as Indo-Iranians, their own name for themselves was Aryas (or Aryans) – the 'noble ones'. There were two waves, the first in around 2000 BC travelling through northern Persia and on to Northwest India. Through time, they ousted the Indus Valley civilisation which had held sway in the region since around the middle of the fourth millennium BC. In around 1500 BC a second wave of Indo-Iranians settled in Persia.

The nomadic Indo-Iranians based their religious beliefs on natural things, viewing their gods not as having human form, but basing them on the natural forces that exert pressures on people – wind, sun, rain and storm.

We know little of what happened to Zoroastrianism in the centuries after Zoroaster's death. The movements of the nomadic tribes certainly must have spread it across the Persian plateau and by the sixth century BC, it was Persia's pre-eminent religion. By that time, the Medes, who had come to power in western Persia in the seventh century, had been supplanted by the Persians.

In 550, Cyrus (r. 559-530 BC), who had been ruler of the small Persian kingdom of Anshan which was located in southwestern Persia, ousted the Median King Astyages (r. 585-550) before going on, in 547 BC, to take prisoner the fantastically wealthy king of Lydia. He next seized power in the huge Babylonian Empire in 539. In just 20 years, Cyrus had created the world's largest empire. Even so, he established a reputation for being fair, just and tolerant in his dealings with his subjects. His descendants espoused the same principles and they also spread Zoroastrianism wherever they went, largely via the Magi, the tribe that provided priests. Even though they had worked on behalf of the Medes, they remained in office during Cyrus's time and long after. They were royal chaplains and whenever a delegation set out to some far-flung corner of the empire on military or diplomatic business, Magi accompanied it. Many also lived in Persian settlements that were established across the empire.

Alexander the Great ended the Achaemenid Empire in 331 BC, destroying the magnificent royal palace of Persepolis and murdering many priests in the process. He and the empire that followed his – the Seleucid – expressed the desire to unite the Persian and Greek cultures but they were hated by Persians who saw them as little more than foreign intruders. The Seleucids were finally thrown out of Persia in the middle of the second century BC by the Parthians, a native Persian dynasty. Nevertheless, the Parthians, whose empire, lasting from 247 BC until 224 BC, was every bit as extensive as that of the Achaemenids, retained many elements of Hellenistic culture, such as its architectural style and some types of coin.

Their empire stretched from North India to Turkey and they stood against Rome, the largest power to do so. By the time Jesus Christ was walking the earth, the Parthians had made Zoroastrianism the world's leading religion.

During the Parthian hegemony, the ancient traditions and sacred literature of Persia began to be collected for the first time. The resulting work was named the *Avesta*. The book is written in the otherwise unrecorded Avestan language and its principal text in the liturgical group is the aforementioned *Yasna*. This name is derived from the *Yasna* ceremony which is the main Zoroastrian act of worship. During it, the *Yasna* text is incanted. The five Gathas are the most important part of the *Yasna*. These consist of seventeen hymns, the composition of which is attributed to Zoroaster. The hymns, as well as five short texts that are also included in the *Yasna*, are in the Old Avestan language, also known as 'Gathic'. The rest of the texts in the *Yasna* are written in Younger Avestan. This derives not only from a later stage of the language's development, but from an entirely different region.

The Muslim Conquest

The Parthians were brought down in 224 AD when a minor ruler – Ardashir I (r. 224-242 AD) from the southwest of Persia rebelled against them. He named his dynasty the Sasanid Empire after one of his ancestors, Sasan, and it remained in power until the arrival of the Muslims in the seventh century. From what they left behind, it is evident that the five centuries or so during which they ruled were a time of splendour and glory for Zoroastrian Persia with the

Zoroastrian religion enjoying a great deal of power in the empire. The high priest was very influential in the creation of imperial policy, the Zoroastrians always emphasising the importance of the unity of church and state.

The Prophet Muhammad died in 633 AD and one year later the Muslims first invaded Persia, initially looting and pillaging, but eventually seeking permanent conquest of the empire, a process that took more than sixteen years. The primary objective, of course, was to spread the word of Muhammad and convert people to Islam and the government of Persia was rapidly islamicised although there were no major efforts initially to convert Persians to Islam. The Zoroastrians were treated as dhimmis – non-Muslim citizens in an Islamic state which gave them certain safeguards and the Arab governors were happy to protect the local Zoroastrian population in exchange for tribute. Through time, however, laws were passed that enforced the view that non-Muslims in Persia were inferior. Zoroastrians were oppressed and poor due to the lack of opportunities for advancement and they also became victims of attacks because of their religion. Economic pressure to convert began to be exerted and the nobility and town dwellers were amongst the first to convert, the practice then spreading further, to the landed gentry and the peasants. Measures were introduced to speed up the process. For example, if a member of a family converted to Islam, he immediately inherited all of the family's property. After the overthrow of the Umayyad caliphate by the Abbasids in 750, Muslim Iranians received better treatment from the new government, both in Iran and in Baghdad. The Abbasids cleverly 'Zoroastrianised' Islam in Iran which rendered it easier for Iranians to convert.

Finally, Zoroastrians, denied education, opportunity and equality, began to migrate to the towns and villages in the great salt deserts, particularly to Yazd and Kerman which, to this day, remain centres of Zoroastrianism. In modern-day Iran, there are now about 25,000 followers of the ancient Persian religion, mainly located in the capital Teheran and on the Yazdi Plain.

There are two main communities of Zoroastrians – those of South Asian background, known as Parsis, and those of Central Asian background. The Parsis are the descendants of the tribes who travelled to Northwest India around 2000 BC and settled there. A census in India in 2011 put the number of Parsis at 57,264. Worldwide, it is estimated that there are between 124,000 and 190,000 Zoroastrians, an imprecise number because of wildly varying estimates of the number in Iran. There are other small communities around the world, taken abroad by the Iranian diaspora.

3

Ancient Greece

'Bear up, my child, bear up; Zeus who oversees
and directs all things is still mighty in heaven.'
Sophocles

Early Greek Religion

Minoan Crete

Greece's ancient history covers a period of about 6,000 years, from the development of agriculture and the establishment of permanent settlements until it became part of the Roman Empire around 27 BC. On the Greek mainland, little evidence has been found of religious practices from the early Bronze Age (c. 3300 BC), but the Cyclades group of islands provides us with marble figurines that appear to have religious significance. Most commonly found are an elongated female figure and a version of this figure in the shape of a violin. They are usually small – less than a foot in height – but some life-size examples have been discovered.

Crete, home to the Minoan culture, is famous for its ancient royal palaces, but until 1979, no religious structures had been found. In that year, an excavation at a site at Anemospilia, near Knossos, uncovered a small Minoan temple which had been destroyed by an earthquake and, surprisingly, it provided evidence of human sacrifice.

The object of Minoan worship seems to have been the bull, and bulls were also sacrificed. There were ceremonies in the central courtyards of palaces in which men leapt over bulls acrobatically, as is evidenced by scenes from wall paintings and on various objects. In the palaces, pillar crypts – subterranean rooms with a central pillar – display the main Minoan religious symbol, the double-axe symbol which is carved on the pillars. This axe was, generally speaking, not a weapon, but was used by woodmen. Earthenware figurines holding snakes have been found, snakes serving as house-guardians which led to them becoming the household goddess's sacred animal.

The Mycenaeans

In the Late Bronze Age (c. 1600-1100) after the demise of the Minoans, the Mycenaeans held sway both on the Greek mainland and on the islands, building massively fortified palaces on high citadels, the main sites being Thebes, Athens, Tiryns, Pylos and Mycenae. During this period, the earliest written texts appear, in the form of a script called 'Linear B'. This archaic form of Greek was finally deciphered in 1952 and, amongst other things, the tablets that have been found contain a list of 'proportional tribute and ritual offerings'. It seems that, as well as 'tributes' and 'offerings', there were people who fulfilled priestly roles, both male and female. There were also gods, one of the most important of whom was Poseidon. A number of other classical deities featured, including Zeus, Hera, Ares, Hermes, Athena, Artemis and Dionysus.

Classical Greek Religion

Around the end of the Bronze Age, the Mycenaean culture was destroyed, possibly by the mysterious 'Sea Peoples', allegedly a seafaring confederation, but of unknown origin. There is a gap then from which very little in the way of pottery has survived. Linear B died and the great palaces and their art fell into ruin. Population declined but alphabetic writing arrived and much of the technology of previous times survived – construction, boat-building, agriculture, weaving, pottery and metallurgy. Greece at this time – around 1100 BC – comprised 158 city states which were all independent of each other, although many were relatively small.

Greek religion consisted, basically, of the worship of 12 gods who lived on Mount Olympus, the highest mountain in Greece. Each deity had different attributes, somewhat reminiscent of today's comic superheroes, although their relationships are more reminiscent of a soap opera:

Zeus
The king of the gods and ruler of Mount Olympus, Zeus was the youngest child of the Titans, Cronus and Rhea, his siblings being Poseidon, Hades, Demeter and Hestia. The Titans were another race of deities that preceded the Olympians. Zeus was the god of the sky, lightning, thunder, law, order and justice and amongst the symbols associated with him were

the thunderbolt, the eagle, the oak tree, the lion, the sceptre and the scales.

Hera

Hera was the queen of the gods, the youngest daughter of Cronus and Rhea and sister-wife of Zeus. She was the goddess of marriage, women and family and symbols associated with her were the peacock, the cuckoo and the cow. She often sought revenge on Zeus's other lovers and their children.

Poseidon

The god of the seas, earthquakes and tidal waves, Poseidon, middle son of Cronus and Rhea, was married to the Nereid Amphitrite – a Nereid being a sea nymph – which did not prevent him from having many lovers, like most of the male gods. His symbols included the horse, the bull, the dolphin and, of course, the trident.

Demeter

Demeter was the goddess of fertility, agriculture, nature and the seasons and her responsibilities were grains and the fertility of the earth. She was associated with the poppy, wheat, the torch, cornucopia and the pig. Mother of Persephone, she was the lover of both Zeus and Poseidon, despite being the middle daughter of Cronus and Rhea and, therefore, their sister.

Athena

Wisdom, knowledge, reason, intelligent activity, literature, handicrafts, science, defence and strategic warfare were in the wide-ranging brief of the goddess Athena, daughter of

Zeus through a liaison with the Oceanid Metis, another sea nymph. The owl and the olive tree were associated with her.

Apollo

Son of Zeus and Leto, daughter of the Titans Coeus and Phoebe, Apollo was the god of light, prophecy, philosophy, inspiration, poetry, music and the arts, as well as medicine and healing. He was born the twin brother of the goddess, Artemis. Symbols included the sun, the lyre, the swan and the mouse.

Artemis

Artemis, Apollo's twin sister, was the goddess of hunting, virginity, archery, the moon and the animals, with symbols including the moon, the horse, the deer, the hound, the she-bear, the snake, the cypress tree and the bow and arrow.

Ares

The dreadful god of war, violence and bloodshed, Ares was the offspring of Zeus and Hera and was hated by all the other gods. His symbols included the boar, the serpent, the dog, the vulture, the spear and the shield.

Aphrodite

Aphrodite was the goddess of love, beauty and desire with symbols including the dove, the bird, the apple, the bee, the swan, the myrtle and the rose. She was the daughter of Zeus and the Oceanid Dione although another version has it that she was born from sea foam after the semen of Uranus dripped into the sea following his castration by his youngest son, Cronus. Despite her marriage to another god,

Hephaestus, she enjoyed numerous affairs, including one with Ares.

Hephaestus

Hephaestus enjoyed the roles of master blacksmith and craftsman of the gods, making all the gods' weapons. He was the god of fire and the forge, associating with fire, the anvil, the axe, the donkey, the hammer and tongs. He was either the son of Zeus and Hera or just Hera on her own and was married to Aphrodite.

Hermes

The god of commerce, communication, borders, eloquence, diplomacy, thieves and games, Hermes served as the messenger of the gods. He was the son of Zeus and the nymph, Maia, and the second-youngest of the gods. Symbols included the caduceus – a staff entwined by two snakes – winged sandals and cap, the stork and the tortoise whose shell he used to invent the lyre.

Hestia

Hestia was the goddess of the hearth, as well as domesticity and the family. She was the oldest child of Cronus and Rhea.

Dionysus

Wine, celebrations and ecstasy were the godly responsibilities of Dionysus, as well as the art of the theatre. Son of Zeus and the human Theban princess, Semele, he married the Cretan princess, Ariadne. He was the youngest god and the only Olympian to have a human mother. Symbols included the grapevine, ivy, the cup, the tiger, the panther, the leopard, the dolphin, the goat, and the pine-cone.

Other gods and goddesses are occasionally included in the Olympian twelve. These include Hades – or Pluto – god of the underworld, the dead and the riches under the earth; Persephone, queen of the underworld and also goddess of springtime; Heracles, the greatest of the Greek heroes; Asclepius, the god of medicine and healing; Eros, the god of sexual love and beauty; and Hebe, the goddess of youth and the cupbearer for the gods, serving them nectar and ambrosia.

At the same time, thousands of local gods existed that became associated with the Olympian deities. It is interesting, however, that the Greeks did not have an exact equivalent to the English word 'religion' and there were no actual priests. Nonetheless, Greek religion was embedded in every facet of life.

Greek gods were often called upon with the use of sacrifice, one of the most important facets of worship. A gift, often the thigh of an animal, was offered to the god by being placed on the altar outside the temple in question. The aim of the sacrifice was either to seek a favour from the god in question or to ask him or her not to do harm. The ritual had to be performed in a rigorously precise fashion or it would be rendered futile. The victim had to be chosen correctly, the method of sacrifice had to be appropriate and all of the cult names of the god had to be used during the ritual. At oracles, sacred sites where gods would answer questions posed by worshippers, sacrifice was carried out first. The gods were everywhere in the home, offerings being made to them when drinking a cup of wine or eating food. A shrine to Hestia, goddess of the hearth, was a common feature in many homes.

Festivals were very frequent in Ancient Greece, the most important of these were the four Pan-Hellenic – and, therefore, national – festivals. Featuring music and athletics competitions, these drew huge crowds of celebrants from a wide area of Greece. Athens enjoyed no fewer than 120 days of festivals a year.

The dark side of Classical Greek religion manifested itself in the worship of the god Dionysus. The Maenads – literally translated as 'raving ones' – as the female worshippers of Dionysus were called, would reach a state of ecstatic frenzy through dancing and the consumption of large quantities of alcohol. At night, they would go into the mountains and practise strange esoteric rites. And curse tablets – *katadesmoi* – have been discovered which have a name inscribed on them in the hope that the named person would fall victim to some terrible fate.

Attitude to Death and the Afterlife

There were also mystery cults, membership of which, one imagines, ensured a good afterlife. But for most Greeks this was not something they could expect. After death, Charon, the boatman, would ferry the soul across the River Styx which marked the boundary between Earth and the Underworld. The Underworld was described as being located at the outer edges of the ocean or beneath the depths or at the end of the Earth and it could not be seen by the living. Guarding the gates of the Underworld and preventing the souls of the dead from leaving, was Cerberus, a monstrous, multi-headed dog. There was also an area in which the Judges of the Underworld decided where to send the arriving souls. They could go to Elysium – a place for those who were especially distinguished; the Fields of Asphodel – a place for ordinary, undistinguished souls; Mourning Fields – for souls who wasted their lives for unrequited love; or Tartarus – a dungeon of torment and suffering.

Temples

Temple styles evolved through time, from Doric to Ionic to Corinthian, each more ornate than the last. They consisted largely of a central hall with a columned porch which was almost always situated at the front, although occasionally there was also one at the rear. There were rows of columns at the back, at the front and sometimes even all round, creating a colonnade. At each end of the pediment, the pitched roof provided a triangular space. This was often decorated with whatever mythological theme was important to the temple.

The temples were never particularly big, most under 30 metres in width and little more than 60 metres in length. Access was easy for large crowds of people, one end being open. Inside would stand a large statue of the particular god that was the subject of worship at that particular temple.

4

Ancient Rome

'Jove lifts the golden balances that show the fates
of mortal men, and things below.'
Homer, *The Iliad*

Borrowing from Greece

The religion of Rome during the period of the Republic (507-27 BC) and the time of the early Empire (27-337 BC) was complex. Romans viewed themselves as highly religious and they would very much have attributed their city's rise to be the world's major power to their piety and their good relations with their gods. The Roman politician and lawyer, Cicero (106-43 BC) expressed the Romans' view of their own piety:

'If we compare ourselves with other peoples, in various things we appear equal or even inferior, except that of religion, meaning the worship of the gods, in which we are far more superior.'

The development of Roman religion was influenced by Greeks who had settled in coastal areas of southern Italy. The Romans adapted Greek myths and iconography to their Latin literature and art, and they even integrated Greek religious practices into their culture. They borrowed Greek gods and made them their own. Thus, the Greek Zeus became the Roman god Jupiter; Venus, a horticultural deity, could be identified with Aphrodite, the Greek goddess of beauty. This appropriation of Greek gods dates back to the fifth century BC but native deities were still worshipped.

Like the Greeks, the Romans had no word equivalent to our English word 'religion'. *Religio* meant 'strict observance of the rites'. They performed rites, carried out sacrifices and staged festivals in order to curry favour with their gods and get something in return. Religion was deeply intertwined with Roman public life and politics and priests – members of the upper classes – were part of the political elite. So, the same men who were elected to public office might also have religious functions. Julius Caesar (100-44 BC), for instance, was *pontifex maximus* – the high priest of the College of Pontiffs – before he was elected consul. Indeed, the link between humans and gods was provided not by priests but by those elected to the Senate or council. They dealt with religious matters and supervised the way people related to the gods.

Augurs interpreted the will of the gods and supervised the delineating of boundaries – a reflection of universal order – which gave divine authority to Rome's expansion, making it a matter of divine destiny. As they expanded the empire throughout the Mediterranean, the Romans were happy to absorb the gods and religions of other peoples rather than extinguish them or force those they had subjected to convert to their religion. The maintenance of tradition, they believed, helped to promote stability and made it easier to incorporate the people of a conquered territory into the Roman Empire. Local deities were worshipped alongside Roman ones and Romans, too, would devote worship to local gods wherever they were.

Foreign deities were worshipped in Rome at the height of the Empire, and they were also carried to far-flung outposts of the Empire. Amongst these were the Anatolian mother goddess Cybele; the Egyptian goddess Isis; the Gaulish goddess of fertility Epona; and the Persian deity Mithras. Romans imported 'mystery' religions in which participation was reserved for initiates. These offered initiates salvation in the afterlife for carrying out secret rituals that would be practised in addition to the normal family rites and public religion. The secrecy of these rites, however, made many Romans suspicious, perhaps believing them to have a subversive purpose and to be a threat to traditional morality. Attempts – sometimes brutal – were made to suppress them. The cult of Bacchus, for instance, worship of whom was orgiastic, was severely restricted by official Senate decree in 186 BC. But there were also mystery cults on behalf of Isis and Osiris from Egypt, and Mithras, the Persian god of light and truth. He became popular with soldiers and traders in particular. He is most often depicted slaying a bull which symbolises his functions as 'saviour from death' and 'warrior'.

From around the time of Emperor Augustus (r. 27 BC-14 AD), a great deal of religious attention was focused on the emperor. The Romans believed that nothing great could be achieved without divine help and successful Romans, therefore, usually associated themselves personally with a god. It was believed, however, that the emperor was a god. This was a great help in establishing stability and unity throughout the empire. The Republic had always resisted the absolute rule that had been exercised by Hellenistic kings, but when Julius Caesar was assassinated in 44 BC, he was listed amongst the gods. Then, when Augustus came to power, his deification was demanded by parts of the Empire, especially in the east, and some places did accord him divine honours. His successor, Tiberius (r. 42 BC-37 AD) declined deification. This angered the Senate which refused to make him a god after his death. After him, however, with the exception of Nero, all the early emperors were declared divine.

Roman Worship

For ordinary Romans, religion was a part of everyday life. Each home boasted a household shrine – the *lararium* – at which prayers could be said and offerings could be made to the family's domestic gods. They worshipped in this context the *Lares* and the *Penates*. The *Lares* were 'spirits of the farmland' and seem to have been associated with ancestors who were buried there; the *Penates* were the spirits who guarded the family larder. They were worshipped alongside Vesta who was the goddess of the private and public hearth.

The rites practised in the home came under the supervision of the paternal head of the household and rituals took place for important events in family life such as the coming of age of the heir. Rome's most famous priesthood consisted of the state-supported Vestal virgins who attended Rome's public hearth for more than a thousand years until they were disbanded when Christianity became the empire's religion. They remained chaste while they performed the role.

Three of the oldest Roman deities – Jupiter, Juno and Minerva – were worshipped in a splendidly large temple on the Capitoline Hill and they are known, consequently, as the 'Capitoline Triad'. The central hall of worship was dedicated to Jupiter and the two other gods had smaller halls to the left and right. Other deities were created over the centuries, according to the requirements or the crises of the time. The cult of Asclepius for instance, was created in response to a plague in 293-291 BC and Cybele was introduced in the face of the threat posed to Rome by Hannibal.

The Edict of Milan

Roman religion was effectively brought to an end by the Edict of Milan, published in 313 AD by the Emperors Licinius (r. 308-324 AD) and Constantine I (r. 306-337 AD). This permitted Christianity to be practised in the Roman Empire and, as the edict said, the Christian church was the only one of the cults competing for the hearts and minds of Romans, to be singled out for 'compensation from our benevolence'. It took nearly another 70 years for the Roman Empire to become officially Christian, but Theodosius I (r. 379-395) had proscribed all other religions by 381 AD.

5

Celtic Religions

Celtic Gods

In the absence of written texts, little is really known of the
ancient Celtic religion. The Celts were a people that spread
across Europe from about 3000 BC but eventually became
absorbed by the Roman Empire. At the very margins of
the Empire – in Scotland, Ireland, Wales and Cornwall –
they clung on and would later exert influence on a type of
Christianity that was very different to that of Rome or Greece.
Each tribe, or clan had its own pantheon of gods, although
there were a few that were widely worshipped and gods from
other cultures (from Rome, for instance) were borrowed.
Warrior heroes were absolutely central to their belief, beings
that possessed supernatural powers. They also believed in the
sacred nature of the earth and the importance of the Earth
Mother who was the goddess of fertility and protection as
well as the bringer of life.

The religion of the Celts had a habit of mingling historical
reality with mythological events. In Ireland, for instance, the
gods were based on the early invaders of Ireland, the Tuatha

Dé Danann ('people/tribe of the goddess Dana or Danu'). They had defeated the Fomorians who represented the destructive force of nature before losing to the Sons of Mil, or Milesians from the northwest of the Iberian Peninsula. The Tuatha retreated underground into the *Sidhe* mounds, an underworld that was halfway between the world of humans and the Otherworld of the gods.

Dagda, 'the father of all', was one of the Tuatha. He is often described as a large man, or even a giant, clad in a cloak. He carries a staff or club, one end of which can kill while the other brings to life. He also has a cauldron that never empties and a magic harp with which he can control men's emotions as well as change the seasons. He is identified with fertility, agriculture, manliness and strength as well as magic, druidry and wisdom. Dagda is the only god that appears throughout the Celtic world.

Being the source of fertility and life, goddesses were even more important to the Celts, particularly the triad of Danu, Macha and Brigid. Brigid, the daughter of Dagda, was responsible for learning, culture and skill and survived into Christianity as St Brigid. She was associated with spring, fertility, healing, poetry and smithcraft and shared many of the attributes of the goddess. Her feast day was originally a pagan festival named Imbolc, at the beginning of spring.

In common with the gods of countless other cultures, the Celtic gods lived in a separate, mythical realm, the Otherworld. This was made up of the *Sidhe* – natural mounds; Tír fo-Thuinn – 'the land under the waves'; Tír na nÓg – 'the land of youth'; and Mag Mell – 'the field of happiness'. The Otherworld was viewed as a land of comfort and contentment where everyone was immortal and anyone wounded in battle on earth would be healed almost immediately. Celtic heroes possessed superhuman powers while remaining human. Cú Chulainn was one of the better known of these, believed to be an incarnation of the god Lugh who was also his father. Christians later interpreted him as Christ battling evil.

Celtic Worship

Celts worshipped not in temples or churches, but out in the open. Human sacrifice and the decapitated heads of enemies played a significant part but, eventually, the Roman authorities put a stop to the practice of embalming the heads and exhibiting them. Celts believed the head had a special power and that owning someone's head meant gaining the ability to possess the power of the deceased. To them it was the seat of the soul and a symbol of divinity and the powers of the Otherworld. The victims of human sacrifice were usually those who had broken the law but, if criminals were in short supply, innocent people would be used. Sacrifices sometimes took the form of burning inside a large wicker man but drowning and hanging were also used. The first-century Greek historian, Diodorus Siculus, wrote about the Druids and human sacrifice:

'These men predict the future by observing the flight and calls of birds and by the sacrifice of holy animals: all orders of society are in their power... and in very important matters they prepare a human victim, plunging a dagger into his chest; by observing the way his limbs convulse as he falls and the gushing of his blood, they are able to read the future.'

As well as performing ceremonies and rituals the Druids were also legal authorities, adjudicators, medical practitioners and political advisers. They were prevented by doctrine, however, from recording their knowledge in written form and, consequently, we have no written accounts of their work or their lives. What we do know we have learned from writings in other cultures, such as the Romans. They were held in such high regard that it was said that they could intervene in a conflict and stop two opposing armies from going to battle.

By the early seventh century, Christianity, brought to Ireland by St Patrick and others, had reduced the Druids to insignificance. The Christianity that developed in Ireland was different to that of the rest of the Roman Empire. Ancient Celtic art styles decorated crosses and manuscripts which were emblazoned with intertwining plants and animals rather than the human form which was the norm in European Christian art. Spiritual guidance (*anamchairdeas*) and austere penance were focused upon and prayer was used for every aspect of daily life, from lighting a fire, to cooking a meal.

Following the departure of the Romans from England, there was a return to paganism. Augustine of Canterbury (early sixth century – c. 604) was sent by Pope Gregory the Great (in office 590-604) to convert the Anglo-Saxons but the north of the country practised the Celtic form of Christianity that had been brought to England by missionaries from Ireland. There were differences in the two – what date Easter should be, for instance – and the Synod of Whitby was convened in 663 to try to resolve these differences. Nonetheless, the Anglo-Saxon Church still exhibited the Celtic style in its manuscript decoration and its missionary practice.

6

Norse Religions

'To Odin many a soul was driven, to Odin
many a rich gift given.'
Snorri Sturluson, *The Heimskringla*, Or,
Chronicle of the Kings of Norway

Origins and Worship

When we think of Norse mythology and religion, we always think of Vikings. They rampaged their way across Europe in the ninth and tenth centuries, but Norse religion dates back to far earlier than that. In fact, the first figures of gods and goddesses that have been found derive from the Scandinavian Bronze Age, around 1600 to 450 BC. The cult of Wodin, or Odin, arrived later, when Celtic and Germanic peoples moved westwards and northwards across Europe between the third and sixth centuries, bringing new religious ideas and cults. Odin would become the principal god in the pantheon worshipped by the Vikings.

Life was undoubtedly harsh for them, living, as they

did, in a dreadful environment and, as is often the case, religion probably helped make sense of such difficult living conditions. But, it also provided them with a justification for their warlike, violent actions. In all things, however, Odin reigned supreme. In Scandinavian mythology, the world was divided into nine separate worlds. Asgard was the realm of the Aesir tribe of gods and goddesses, amongst whom were Odin himself, Frigg, Baldr and Tyr. Midgard was the home of humans. Through these nine worlds grew a World Tree, Yggdrasil, usually depicted as a giant ash tree whose roots reach into spirit worlds never entered by humans. At the foot of the tree sat the Three Fates of Destiny, the Norns. These were sometimes thought to be more powerful even than the gods and goddesses because they were responsible for spinning the threads of life and decided the fate of every human. The Tree was the source of unborn souls and so was itself linked with the fate of human beings.

Midgard was constantly threatened by evil, darkness and chaos, and there was a perpetual struggle to keep these forces at bay. The Vikings' harsh environment no doubt helped them to imagine frost giants, living in the world of Jötunheimr. These huge beings menaced the humans in Midgard as well as the gods in Asgard by throwing ice and snow at them. One of the Aesir gods, Thor the great thunderer and god of fertility, often entered Jötunheimr in order to kill the giants with his great hammer which he named Mjölnir. Vikings would paint an image of Mjölnir on barn doors to protect them from evil spirits and they began to wear the hammer as a symbol, in the same way that Christians wear the crucifix.

Old Norse religion was based around ritual practice, kings and chiefs playing a major role in this and undertaking public acts of sacrifice. Outdoor spaces initially provided the places of worship, but by the third century AD, there were purpose-built buildings in which they worshipped. They consulted with shaman-like figures, practitioners of the sorcery known as Seiðr.

The Vikings both buried and cremated their dead, usually accompanied by a variety of gifts. They believed that those who died of sickness or old age would be welcomed into the kingdom of Hel which was presided over by a creature of the same name. She was the daughter of the god Loki and was appointed to her role by Odin. She has been described as half blue and half flesh-coloured, with a gloomy appearance. Her domain was a dark place with a wickerwork of writhing serpents on the walls. In the banqueting hall, the knife was called 'hunger' and the plate 'starvation'. Warriors who were killed on the battlefield were rescued by Valkyries, maidens who chose who would live or die in battle. The dead warriors were taken to Valhalla, the afterlife hall of the slain where they enjoyed feasts and fought mock battles.

Ragnarok and the Coming of Christianity

In Norse mythology, Ragnarok is a series of events that will take place in the future. These include a huge final battle that will end in the deaths of many important gods, including Odin, Thor, Tyr, Freyr, Heimdallr and Loki. Disasters are foretold including the submersion of the world in water after which it will re-emerge, refreshed and fertile. Two humans, Lif and Lifthrasir, will repopulate the world and they will not worship the old Aesir gods, but God Almighty who lives in Gimlé, the paradise above all else. Undoubtedly, this represents the merging of Viking mythology with Christianity which was flourishing across northern Europe. By the twelfth century, Christianity had supplanted the old Norse religion.

7

Religions of the Nomads

'They worship only the following gods, namely Hestia,
whom they reverence beyond all the rest, Zeus and Earth,
whom they consider to be the wife of Zeus; and after these
Apollo, Celestial Aphrodite, Heracles and Ares.'

Herodotus, *On the Scythians*

The Scythians

The Iranian people, the Scythians, inhabited the western and
central Eurasian Steppes from around the ninth century BC
until around the first century BC. Known as the Eurasian
Nomads, they were an important race, with territory that,
by the seventh century BC, stretched from modern-day
Romania to Turkestan. They were the first people from the
East to communicate with the West, and ideas on religion,
art and other matters were exchanged between the two.

From the Greek historian Herodotus (c. 484-25 BC), in
his *History of the Persian Wars*, we have learned about the
religion of the Scythians. The major gods they appear to have

worshipped were the Sky Father, Papaios, whose wife was Api, Mother Earth. There were also gods of fire and war but the Scythians did not create images of their deities or build temples to them. Annual sacrifices were made to them, however, in which horses were the customary victims. After the animals were strangled, their meat was cooked on a fire made of their bones and a chunk of that meat was tossed into the fire as an offering. The Scythian god of war was represented by an iron sword that was raised on a pile of brushwood and he was the recipient of large numbers of cattle and horses in sacrifices. Captives taken in battle were also sacrificed to him, and their blood poured over the sword of the god.

The death of a king was ceremonially celebrated, his body being processed through all the villages over which he had ruled, his wives and servants following the wagon on which his body lay. Burial for him was in a wooden chamber and a few servants were strangled and left in the chamber with his body when it was sealed so that they could accompany him on his onward journey. The bones of horses and dishes made of gold have also been found in these chambers.

The Mongols

The Mongol people can be traced back to the Donghu, which was a nomadic tribal confederation inhabiting eastern Mongolia and Manchuria. They defeated the Turkic peoples who had been dominant in Mongolia and began to build an empire that by the thirteenth and fourteenth centuries, was the greatest the world had ever seen, stretching from the Amur River that now marks the border between the

Russian Far East and Northeastern China, to the Volga that flows through central Russia and into the Caspian Sea.

The principal deity of the Mongols was Tengri which as well as being the god's name was also their word for the blue sky and for everything that was good. People worshipped him in a solitary way, bowing to him on the summits of mountains. They burned incense of juniper in tribute to him but, like other nomadic deities, he was not represented visually. Tengri, however, was not responsible for creation; according to the Mongols, the world was made by two creators – one good, one evil. There were 99 'tengri' gods who protected the nomads' all-important herds. Success in breeding horses was guaranteed by reverence for the deity Ataga tengri, for instance, while other tengris were responsible for the protection of cows and yaks.

The Mongols worshipped geographical phenomena such as lakes, rivers and mountains, passes and mountain tops, believing these to host spirits. Travellers in such areas, had to placate the spirits to ensure safe passage. This was done by adding a stone to a cairn known as an *obo*. Libations would also be poured in order to propitiate Mother Earth.

Mongols made offerings to their great leaders, especially Genghis Khan (r. 1206-1227) who was believed to be of heavenly origin. Horses were dedicated to him and he was sometimes associated with Tengri himself. Leaders of the tribes were believed to have shamanic powers, called upon to cure illnesses and heal wounds, their secret knowledge coming to them while in a state of trance. The shaman cast out evil spirits and performed all sacrificial rituals.

The Slavic Peoples and Religion

The Slavs originated in Eurasia, but from the early sixth century, they spread to Central, Eastern and Southeastern Europe. What little we know of their religion derives from those Slavs who lived east of the River Elbe although the exact nature of it is still subject to conjecture. The best-known Slavic deity seems to have been Perun, the god of thunder and lightning, similar to the Norse god Thor. In around 980, Vladimir the Great, Grand Prince of Kiev (r. 980-1015), a ruler of Viking descent, built a pagan temple to six gods in Kiev. These were Perun; the Slav gods Stribog and Dažbog, father and son and each representing the sun and fire; Mokosh, who was a goddess of Mother Nature and of Finno-Ugric origin; and Khors and Simargi, deities of Iranian origin.

A representation of Perun on a hill outside Vladimir's palace showed him resplendent with a head of silver and a bronze beard. Sacrifices, both of cattle and people were carried out for him and it is likely that his emergence as a deity was influenced by the worship of Thor in Scandinavia, since Kiev was, at the time, a Viking state.

Temples have been found in the western Slavic area where the pagan religion remained in place until 1168 when King Valdemar I of Denmark (r. 1131-82) destroyed the temple in Arkona which was situated on the island of Rügen in what is now Germany. The Slavs had in all likelihood been influenced by the Germans in their construction of places of worship dedicated to their gods. The temple at Arkona could only be entered by the priest who made sacrifices inside and practised divination. One of the main Slavic deities was the god of war, Svetovid, who was depicted with several heads, two looking forward and two back. In temples near Stettin, the god Triglav was depicted as three-headed, sometimes with the heads of goats and often with gold blindfolds over his eyes. The heads represented the sky, the earth and the underworld and the blindfolds were to ensure that he was unable to see people's sins. Multi-headed gods can be said to be intrinsically Slavic.

The Religion of Latvia, Lithuania and the Baltic Prussians

In Latvia, Lithuania and the land of the Baltic Prussians, the old religion was practised until comparatively recently. It was only in the eighteenth century that the sacred groves of Latvia, about which not a great deal is known, were destroyed. In Latvia, worship of the deity Perkons (Lithuania: Perkunas), god of thunder and fertility who was associated with the Slavic god, Perun, continued until 1750. As Lithuania was not Christianised until the fifteenth century – one of the last pagan countries in Europe to adopt Christianity – indigenous religions were still being practised well into the nineteenth century.

Baltic religions were closely related to the original Indo-European religion of India and what was then Persia (now Iran). The god Dievs, the supreme god in the Baltic mythology, is probably derived from the Indian god Dyaus Pita, 'Father Heaven', and Perkunas can be taken back to Parjanya, the Vedic god of the rain.

The Baltic religions have a number of female deities –

Zemes Mate (Mother of the Earth) and Uguns Mate (the Fire Mother) amongst them. Laima and Mara were also important goddesses.

8

Pre-Colombian American Religions

'...they have an idol that they petition for victory in war;
another for success in their labours; and so for everything in
which they seek or desire prosperity, they have their idols,
which they honour and serve.'

Hernan Cortes, about the Aztecs,
in a letter to King Charles V

Before the Spaniards

The period prior to the conquest of Central and South America
by the Spanish in the sixteenth century is often described as
'Pre-Colombian' America. During this period in Central
America, highly developed cultures emerged in areas such
as modern-day Mexico, Guatemala, the central Andes, Peru
and the highlands of Bolivia and in these regions polytheistic
worship was practised. Religion could be divided into two
types, however – that of the ordinary citizens who worshipped
and made offerings at local shrines and the religion of the state
which involved great temples and a highly organised theology.

The Olmecs

In Central America, between about 1200 and 500 BC, a people named the Olmecs by archaeologists, lived on Mexico's Gulf Coast. Their religious tendencies were manifested by the construction of temple communities such as the one at La Venta in the modern Mexican state of Tabasco. This complex is home to a series of buried offerings and tombs and there are also monumental sculptures to be found between mounds and platforms made of sand and clay. It must be presumed that in the distant past, these platforms were the base for wooden structures. At the south end of the complex stands a clay pyramid.

The wild cat, the jaguar, appears to have been central to the worship of the Olmecs. At La Venta, for instance, mosaic pavements have been unearthed that depict the stylised face of the jaguar, possibly an offering to the creature. The jaguar is also evident in a mask found on the lid of a stone coffin. It is shown with a forked tongue, like that of a snake, and with feathers for his eyebrows. There appears to be some association in this with the Aztec god, Quetzalcoatl, a being that is often represented as a plumed serpent. This amalgamation of different animals to create the figure of one god is common to many Central American figures of devotion. The jaguar of the Olmecs also occasionally took human form and in a carving found at Potrero Nuevo this type of figure is seen copulating with a woman. From this union emerged a race of half-human, half-jaguar beings, the human elements usually shown in a paunch and short, stubby limbs. Fangs, claws and a snarling mouth are taken from the jaguar and given to these outlandish creatures. It is believed that they were possibly deities and that they may have represented fertility.

The Maya

After the Olmecs, came the Maya, who inhabited southeastern Mexico, Guatemala, Belize and the western parts of El Salvador and Honduras. The state religion of these people was based on ceremonial centres that were home to temples for worship and ritual acts. Early temples date from around 200 BC, and examples have been found in a Guatemalan rainforest at Tikal and Uaxactun in the department of El Peten in northern Guatemala. What is recognised as the 'Classic Period' of Maya culture took place between 300 AD and 900 AD and during this time the state religion developed fully before fading away after 900.

Maya religion was, quite simply, an agreement between gods and humans. Humans prayed for rain or good crops and the gods, duly satisfied that proper deference had been paid, supplied what was needed to live. Ceremony played a large part in this and, prior to such an event, people had to remain celibate. Husbands and wives slept apart from each other and there would be fasting and confession. Sacrifice was hugely important to Maya religious practice. This could take the form of the worshipper's blood or that of animals or other humans. Famously, in human sacrifice, the heart was extracted from the sacrificial victim while he or she was still alive. For the rain gods, small offerings were preferred or, in human sacrifice, children.

The Mayan deities displayed a blend of human and animal characteristics. They were both good and bad and they also had a sexual duality. They were ambiguous, too, as to which category they fell into. The sun god, for instance, as well as being a god of the sky, was also considered one of the nine lords of the night and the underworld because at night he passed through the underworld on his way back to the east to rise again in the morning.

In the Valley of Mexico, about 40 kilometres northeast of modern-day Mexico City, around the time when the Maya were pre-eminent in the region, the great city of Teotihuacan stood. The city was invaded and sacked in the seventh or eighth century, or possibly even destroyed in an internal uprising but it is home to many of the most important Mesoamerican pyramids of Pre-Colombian America. It hosts many substantial temples on the walls of which can be found a great deal of religious imagery including numerous representations of the rain-god, Chaac – 'the one who makes things grow'. He was evidently of great importance to the Maya. Quetzalcoatl also again appears at Teotihuacan. His image on a temple façade, surrounded by sea shells, suggests that he may have been the god of the waters.

The Toltecs

Toltec culture dominated a nation that centred on Tula in the modern Mexican state of Hidalgo from 900 to 1168 AD. Toltec history, as relayed by the later Aztecs, is the subject of debate and it is thought that it contains a great deal of mythology. The semi-mythological fifth king of the Toltecs, Ce Acatl, was a religious figure who assumed the name Quetzalcoatl after the god. He was exiled by those who worshipped the god Tezcatlipoca and travelled with his followers to Chichen Itza in modern-day Yucatan in Mexico, where he is said to have founded a city and had the massive pyramid, El Castillo, constructed. The centuries had brought change to religion in the region and El Castillo and the other main Toltec pyramid, the Temple of the Morning Star at Tula, each boasted a large colonnaded hall at the foot of their steps where warriors could assemble at religious festivals and ceremonies. They would use their own altars and sacrificial stones, signifying the greater degree of militarism that prevailed at the time. The theocracy had been replaced with a more militaristic rule.

Quetzalcoatl was a sky god to the Toltecs and there was another deity – part eagle and part jaguar – that was a heavenly representation of the warrior class. It fed the sun and the morning star with hearts and blood that were obtained from human sacrifice. A number of the important constituents of Aztec religion can be traced back to the Toltecs. The two civilisations shared a connection between king and warrior, and fire, sun and the morning star were important symbols in both their religious practices. The Toltec method of sacrificing humans was also maintained by the Aztecs, the unfortunate victim being restrained against a low stone platform before his chest was sliced open with a knife and the heart ripped out.

The Aztecs

The Aztecs were dominant in central Mexico from 1300 to 1521, after the Mexica, Texcoca and Tepaneca peoples merged to establish the Aztec Empire. The centre of the empire was the Valley of Mexico in the middle of the modern-day country, around modern-day Mexico City and the eastern part of the State of Mexico. The Aztecs arrived in the valley late in the twelfth century and began the construction of their capital, Tenochtitlan, in the second half of the fourteenth century. They also began to expand their empire around this time.

The Aztecs believed that everything was created by two beings, Ometecuhtli and Omeciuatl – Lord and Lady of the Duality, respectively. These beings were said to have created the gods and human beings but, by the time the Spaniards arrived, they were less prevalent and had been replaced to a large extent by younger, more dynamic deities. The gods, the Aztecs believed, created the earth but the most important element of this was the birth of the sun at Teotihuacan, born following the self-sacrifice of one god. The other gods followed his example and the requisite amount of sacrificial blood was obtained in order to make the sun begin its journey across the heavens. The movement of the sun depended on it being fed with human blood, and sacrifice became viewed as a sacred duty. To that end, numerous human sacrificial victims were required, mostly prisoners of war, amounting to around 20,000 a year.

The sun was personified by the Aztec tribal god Huitzilopochtli who was also the god of the Aztec warriors. The rain god, Tlaloc, was also the god of the peasants and he was regarded as being on the same level as Huitzilopochtli, and their priests were treated as equal to each other. The sun played a part when an Aztec warrior was killed in battle or when a woman died in childbirth. They were believed to join the sun in the sky for a period of four years following which they were reborn as hummingbirds that would follow the sun as it passed through the heavens. The souls of almost anyone else who died went to Mictlan, the Aztec underworld, where they spent four years making the difficult journey from the first level to the ninth, overcoming challenges on the way. The souls of the drowned went to Tlalocan, a paradise that was ruled over by the rain god Tlaloc and his wife Chalchiuhtlicue.

Other Religions

At Chavin de Huantar, a stone-built temple in the northern highlands of Peru, the worship of a supernatural feline developed between 600 and 300 BC. The cult spread across Peru. The cat, jaguar-like but with a human form, can be seen in a tall standing stone on which its shape is carved. The eyebrows and hair of the creature are snakes and the expression on its face has earned it the name 'The Smiling God'.

The Chavin religion was revived in the first millennium AD by the Moche people who lived on the north Peruvian coast. Pottery produced by them depicted humans with fangs and snake belts, often fighting a part-human, part-animal monster. Offerings of human sacrifices were made to the cat-like beings. Other animal gods also existed.

The extensive ruins of the city of Tiahuanaco in western Bolivia are home to many ceremonial buildings that were constructed between 200 and 500 AD, a period during which the city enjoyed a great deal of power and influence. On a monolithic gateway – the 'Gate of the Sun' – can be seen a carving of what appears to be the city's principal god – a standing figure which holds a staff in each hand on which are eagle-headed emblems. Six puma heads constitute his headdress and hanging gruesomely from his belt are the human heads that associate him with human sacrifice.

Meanwhile, between 1200 AD and the year of their conquest by the Incas, the Chimu established a state on the coast of northern Peru. The main object of worship for them was the moon, believed to be even more powerful than the sun because she could be seen during the day as well as at night. A few constellations were also highly regarded and the sea – Ni – was extremely important to them, especially as it provided them with food in the form of fish. Offerings of white maize flour and red ochre were made in order to safeguard the fish supply and to protect the locals from the perils of the sea.

The Incas

Although the pastoral tribe, the Incas, had been established in the area around the city of Cusco since about the twelfth century, it was not until the fifteenth century that they had firmly established their empire, which covered an area of around a million square kilometres. As had happened previously, local worship was practised alongside the state religion. Around Cusco alone, there were numerous Inca shrines which took a wide variety of forms, from natural features to temples that had been specially built. The state religion of the empire was a means of organising the empire, in particular the supply of food, rather than a matter of spirituality. Before anything could be done, from planting crops to going to war, a ritual divination had to be performed and sacrifices were made on such occasions, mostly of such things as maize beer or food, but occasionally of virgins and children.

Pachacuti, emperor of the Incas from 1438 until 1471 or 1472, championed a god named Viracocha (sometimes Huiracocha) who was the creator, and had made the moon, the sun, other deities and humanity. Pachacuti considered him the source of everything and the other deities were there merely to help him. The sun, however, was of paramount importance to the Incas, a male god known as Inti, who was responsible for ensuring that the crops grew.

One fundamental difference between the Inca religion and other Central American forms of worship was that the Incas developed an ancestor cult, making substantial offerings of food and drink to the dead and keeping mummies of their dead emperors in the royal palace that were brought out and paraded at festivals. After death, the Incas believed, those who had been good went to an upper world – Janaq Pacha – a place not unlike the world they had just left behind. Meanwhile, those who had led a sinful life were sent to the lower world – Uku Pacha – a cold place where they were given only stones to eat.

Of course, the Spanish conquest of 1532 wiped away the

old Inca religion, as Roman Catholicism was forced on the indigenous people. Nonetheless, vestiges of it remain to this day amongst those people.

Religions of India

9

Hinduism

'We worship the three-eyed One (Lord Shiva) Who is fragrant and Who nourishes well all beings; may He liberate us from death for the sake of immortality even as the cucumber is severed from its bondage (to the creeper).'
Hindu prayer

A Diverse, Flexible and Evolving Religion

The term 'Hinduism' was coined in the nineteenth century by non-Indians to describe a group of Indian religions, and only then did the diverse beliefs and practices that made up religious life in South Asia begin to be acknowledged as a world religion. The Hindu religion is now the biggest religion of the Indian subcontinent and, after Christianity and Islam, is the world's third-largest religion. The name is derived from the Persian word 'hindu' – *sinhu* in Sanskrit – which means 'Indian'. Around 80 per cent of Indians – about 960 million people – regard themselves as Hindu and around the world it is estimated there are around 30 million more Hindus. Apart from India, Hindus are found in places such as Nepal, Sri Lanka, Indonesia, Bangladesh, Malaysia, Mauritius, Pakistan, the Philippines, the United Kingdom and the United States. Unlike other major religions, it has no single person that can be recognised as its founder, it has no real unified system of belief and there is no notion of salvation or a centralised authority such as the Roman Catholic Vatican. Indeed, diversity would appear to be the only unifying thing about Hinduism, a religion that dates back beyond the second millennium before Christ, although it has no identifiable starting point.

Perhaps the secret of Hinduism's success has been its ability to evolve through the centuries. The Indian subcontinent has been subject to dynamic change and growth over the centuries as different cultures have become predominant, from the Mauryans to the Guptas to the Mughals. Different peoples from different regions have brought their beliefs and their cultural practices to bear on India and Hinduism has evolved as necessary to adapt to these new ideas, cultures and institutions.

Origins

The history of Hinduism can really be broken down into five disparate periods. The Vedic Period, lasting from 1500 BC to 500 BC, brought the compilation of the earliest scriptures, the Vedas, and the emergence of the priesthood. The Classical or Golden Age (500 BC to 500 AD) brought the compilation of a fresh batch of scriptures that incorporated important literary and devotional responses to the emerging faiths of

Buddhism and Jainism, and reliance on the ritual of the fire sacrifice was reduced. Temple worship became more common at this time, the notion of *karma* developed and the discipline of yoga became formalised. In the Medieval Period, from 500 to 1500, a network of great regional temples was constructed in which *bhakti*, the worship of major deities, began. Sanskrit became established as a culturally unifying language and Hindus began to welcome the notion of equality for all worshippers. In the pre-Modern period – from 1500 to 1750 – the city of Pune became a seat of religious learning and there was a growing devotional focus on a 'God without qualities' (*Nirguna Brahman*) in northern India. Finally, during the British Raj, from around 1750 to 1947, what has been termed the Hindu Renaissance began. Reformers, exploiting antipathy to British rule in India, recommended a return to 'eternal law', the expunging of superstitions, and a focus on ethical principles, Indian nationalism and missionary work.

The earliest evidence of prehistoric religion to be found in India dates from the Mesolithic era. It can be seen in rock paintings in the Bhimbetka rock shelters that date to perhaps 30,000 BC or even older. The first evidence of Hinduism, however, was found along the banks of the Indus River, dating to between 2500 BC and 1500 BC, the time when the Indus Valley civilisation was prevalent. The people who lived there had a highly sophisticated society, with an urban culture, drainage and waste disposal facilities and they made superb pottery. Their farming was well developed and they had large granaries to store their surplus grain. Although little is known of the religion of these people, figurines have been uncovered that seem suggestive of later Hindu gods such as Shiva and the mother goddess. The Hindu *linga*, an abstract representation of Shiva, has been found in the ruins of the ancient city of Harappa while other pre-Hindu artefacts such as seals have been found. It is claimed by some that the people of the Indus Valley worshipped a mother goddess who symbolised fertility and, indeed, such worship continues in the Hindu religion in rural areas today. However, the Indus Valley civilisation has left us no buildings that appear to have a religious purpose or signs of elaborate burial rituals.

After the decline of the Indus Valley people, it is thought that the Aryans replaced them, their culture lasting from around 1750 to 500 BC. The Hindu religion evolved during the ensuing centuries of Aryan civilisation. The Aryans were Indo-European invaders or perhaps just migrants, pastoralists arriving from the Caucasus who moved south to settle in the subcontinent. A branch of the Indo-Aryan people, their roots stretch back to the Sintashta culture of the northern Eurasian steppe which lasted from 2100 BC to 1800 BC and which practised funeral sacrifices bearing similarities to the sacrificial funeral rites to be found in the Rig Veda, the ancient collection of Vedic Sanskrit hymns. These Vedic tribes wandered around Northwest India but after the introduction of iron, around 1100 BC, they began to settle in the western Ganges Plain and became agrarian. Basic states began to emerge, the Kuru Kingdom being the most significant. Their culture collected the Vedic hymns and initiated new rituals.

The Aryans spoke Sanskrit and our information about them has been gleaned from the early Sanskrit compositions known as the Vedas, a body of texts that was added to and changed over a period of hundreds of years and that is the very foundation of the Hindu religion. The earliest Vedas were liturgical in nature and were to be used in rituals involving sacrifice to early gods such as Agni, the fire god, and Soma who was the god of plants. Into a sacrificial fire would be thrown a variety of things, from animals to milk and grain. These ceremonies would be managed by specialists who were the elite of Vedic society, priests known as *Brahmins* who sat at the top of a society that was divided into four levels or *varnas*. After the *Brahmins* came the *Kshatriyas*, the ruling and military elite; they were followed by the *Vaishyas* – commoners or peasants engaged in farming. Along with the *Brahmins* and the *Kshatriyas*, the *Vaishyas* were said to be *dvija* or 'twice-born'. This meant that the male members of the family had undergone the sacrament of initiation, confirming their position as full members of society. The fourth *varna* was made up of *Shudras* – the servant class – who did not undergo initiation.

Aryan culture soon dominated North India and the Brahmanical ideology became prevalent everywhere. Ritual and the duties of the king became important to society and maintaining order and living in the right way – *dharma* – governed individual behaviour. Failure to observe the strictures of *dharma* was likely to bring problems both socially and personally. Good *dharma* was related to moral and ritual behaviour and this was defined according to one's *varna* and stage of life, or *ashrama*.

Another set of texts was developed in the later Vedic period. These were the Aranyakas and the Upanishads. They were less concerned with ritual and more with the gaining of spiritual knowledge. Key to this were the notions of *samsara*, *karma*, *dukkha* and *moksha*. *Samsara* meant that all beings were reincarnated time and time again; *karma* is the sum of all the actions in our lives; *dukkha* is the suffering or pain of everyday life caused by the process of endless rebirth; and *moksha* is liberation from the cycle of birth and rebirth and ignorance which can be gained by self-realisation and self-knowledge. Therefore, spiritual knowledge became the aim of Hindus and it became recognised that self-discipline and perhaps asceticism were required to gain it. It can be seen in those who renounce the world and its customs and practices and in the practice of yoga, for example.

India's Golden Age

The period during which the ancient peoples, the Guptas and the Pallavas ruled, brought a golden age to India. Power was centralised and long-distance trade flourished, the law became standardised and literacy increased. Brahman culture was revived by the patronage of the Gupta dynasty who ruled in the north between the third and sixth centuries AD and who happened to be *Vaishnavas*, worshippers of Vishnu. The first Hindu temples, dedicated to the gods, were built. In order to consolidate their dynasty, the Guptas championed the new Puranic Hinduism that had emerged from the Puranas, texts written around that time covering a wide variety of topics, but featuring myths, legends and traditional folktales. These had the aim of spreading Hinduism amongst illiterate people and backward tribes. Scholarship flourished at this time, Hindu philosophy schools emerged and Sanskrit literature blossomed, with writing on a wide range of subjects including medicine, veterinary science, mathematics, astrology, astronomy and astrophysics. Gupta society was organised in accordance with Hindu beliefs which enforced a strict caste or class system.

The Pallavas established a dynasty in the south of the subcontinent that lasted from the fourth until the ninth century. They built some extremely important Hindu temples and academies in places such as Kanchipuram, Mamallapuram, and a number of great Sanskrit poets were writing during this period.

After the decline of the Gupta Empire and the subsequent collapse of the Harsha Empire (606-647) that succeeded it, power was no longer centralised in India. Instead, a number of larger states were established with smaller states paying tribute to them. Religion, too, was regionalised and local cults and languages became more important, leading to a decrease in the influence of Brahmanic Hinduism. This led to competition amongst religious movements for the favour of the local ruler. Meanwhile, around the eighth century, Buddhism began to lose its following in India and gradually disappeared. Puranic Hinduism became the most popular religion on the subcontinent, and local religions and traditions were assimilated into it. Vishnu and Shiva became the most important deities along with Shakti and Deva. Brahmanism was transformed into Puranic Hinduism after the Guptas, resulting in the emergence of a mainstream Hinduism that supplanted all previous traditions.

Medieval Hinduism (c. 1200-c. 1500)

In the early seventh century, Islam arrived in India, brought to the subcontinent by Arab traders and the establishment of Islamic rule in the twelfth century began to impact Indian religions. Buddhism declined dramatically and Hindus were subject to religious violence. The homes and land of Hindu families were appropriated and many were enslaved, sold in the cities of the Delhi Sultanate or sent to Central Asia. Others were forced to convert to Islam in order to preserve or gain their freedom. Many Hindu temples were also destroyed.

In the midst of all of this, Hinduism was undergoing changes. Followers of the Bhakti movement, the spiritual devotional movement that reached its peak between the fifteenth and seventeenth centuries, and that worshipped different gods and goddesses, turned to more accessible avatars such as Krishna and Rama. Thinkers began to treat the teachings of the Upanishads, the Epics, the Puranas and the schools of Hindu philosophy as a single entity.

The Early Modern Era (c. 1500-1850)

The Mughals came to power in India in 1526 and ruled until 1857. Islam was their official state religion and Hinduism remained under pressure during the reigns of Babur (r. 1526-30) and Humayun (r. 1530-40). Hinduism became prominent during the reign of the Hindu King Hemu (r. 1556) who defeated Akbar's (r. 1556-1605) Mughals in the Battle of Delhi and reigned for just a month, although he had been Chief Minister and general supervisor of the Mughal state from 1553. Often, however, during the Mughals' hegemony, subjects were free to worship as they pleased, although non-Muslim men had to pay *Jizya*, a poll tax levied by the government. Those paying were dubbed *dhimmis*, non-Muslim citizens of the Islamic state. *dhimmis* were restricted in some ways, but their rights were fully protected and they enjoyed equality in the laws of property, contract and obligation.

Under Akbar, Humayun's successor, *Din-i-Ilahi* (Faith of God) was introduced as the state religion – a strange amalgam of Islam, Zoroastrianism, Hinduism, Jainism and Christianity. Akbar even abolished the *Jizya* and displayed remarkable tolerance towards religions of all persuasions. Naturally, all of this proved very unpopular with the Muslim clergy, but several of his successors persevered with this policy. Aurangzeb, however, who ruled from 1658 until 1707, was a devout Sunni Muslim and the moderation previously shown towards non-Muslims vanished when he came to the throne. He mounted campaigns against India's non-Muslim states – the Sikhs in the Punjab, the remaining Hindu Rajputs and the Maratha rebels.

The Hindu Marathas, living in the western part of the Deccan, had managed to resist the Mughals and, indeed, led by their ambitious ruler, Shivaji (r. 1674-1680), began to raid Mughal territory. Having made considerable territorial gains, Shivaji was declared emperor (*Chhatrapati*) in 1674. Much of central India was in their hands by Shivaji's death in 1680. Ruled by *Brahmin* prime ministers – *Peshwas* – it flourished and Pune, the capital city, became a centre of Hindu cultural achievement and learning. At its zenith, the Maratha Empire extended from Tamil Nadu in the south of India to Peshawar in the north, now the capital of the province of Khyber Pakhtunkhwa in Pakistan. They would have expanded further, possibly into Afghanistan, but for defeat by the Afghan Durrani Empire in the Third Battle of Panipat in 1761. Ten years later, however, their hegemony over North India was restored by the young Peshwa, Madhravao I (r. 1761-1772).

In order to govern his vast empire effectively, Madhravao gave semi-autonomy to his strongest noblemen and created a kind of confederacy of Maratha states. The Marathas remained the dominant power in India until they were finally defeated by troops of the British East India Company in the Second Anglo-Maratha War that lasted from 1803 to 1805. With the British now in charge of India, Christian missionaries began to arrive and there were many new converts to Christianity.

Modern Hinduism (1850 to the present day)

In the nineteenth century, there was something of a 'Hindu Renaissance', led by a number of reformers who helped to create a perception of Hinduism as a rational, ethical religion. Amongst these activists was Ram Mohan Roy (1772-1833) who, with Dwarkanath Tagore (1794-1846), established the influential Brahmo Samaj reform movement at Calcutta in August 1828, aiming to reform the Brahmanism of the time. The movement also pioneered religious, social and educational improvements within the Hindu community.

Another reformer, Dayananda Saraswati (1824-83), founder of the organisation Arya Samaj, championed a return to the Vedic religion of the time before the Puranas and the Epics, with the emphasis on an eternal, omnipotent and impersonal god and the 'eternal law' (*sanatana dharma*). Behind these two movements was the desire to remove superstition from Hinduism but they also marked the beginning of Indian nationalism.

The Indian mystic and yogi, Paramahamsa Ramakrishna (1836-86) declared the unity of all religions and his disciple,

Vivekananda (1863-1902) developed his teachings and spoke of a united India, an idea developed by Mohandas Gandhi (1869-1948) and others who demanded independence for India. Much of Gandhi's inspiration was drawn from Hindu teachings, especially the notion of *ahimsa* (non-violence). Around the time of the struggle for independence, the term 'Hindu' became political and the concept of *hinditva* ('Hinduness') was coined by VD Savarkar (1883-1966) in an effort to create a collective Hindu identity.

After the partition of India in 1947, the creation of Pakistan and the terrible bloodshed that ensued, Indian nationalist tendencies increased and it began to be perceived as a Hindu country, Hinduism being seen as a specifically Indian religion. These perceptions still prevail and over the decades since independence have led to frequent communal violence.

The true nature of Hindu identity became vaguer after independence, however, with the migration to Britain and America of large numbers of Hindus. The new Hindu communities that began to emerge abroad were supported by gurus and holy men travelling to the West. They occasionally started movements that attracted the attention of Westerners – Transcendental Meditation, for example, which was practised in the late 1960s by celebrities such as The Beatles who contributed to its popularity. Similarly, the Hare Krishna movement flourished after celebrities such as George Harrison became interested in it. Western followers of the religion were drawn to it by its non-sectarian spiritual elements. Meanwhile, by 2000, Hindu communities were well-established abroad and temples such as the magnificent BAPS Shri Swaminarayan Mandir in London – also known as the Neasden Temple – were being built. Issues for modern

Hindus in these countries remain, however – how to deal with caste, intermarriage and attitudes to women.

The Different Schools of Hinduism

Shaivism

Also known as Saivism or Shavism, Shaivism is the sect within the Hindu religion that worships the god, Shiva. One of the principal deities of Hinduism, Shiva is known as the 'destroyer of evil and the transformer' within the Trimurti, the Hindu trinity that also includes Brahma and Vishnu. Shiva creates, protects and transforms the universe. He is often seen with a serpent around his neck, a crescent moon, the holy River Ganga flowing from his matted hair, a third eye on his forehead, the *trishula* – a type of trident – as his weapon and the *damaru*, a small, two-headed drum. He is often depicted, standing on one leg and dancing in the form of the multi-armed *Natarja*, this being the cosmic representation of Shiva's various dance forms. It is an image that is synonymous with Hinduism to many outside the faith. The Katha Upanishad says of Shiva: 'In his robe are woven heaven and earth... He is the bridge from death to deathless life.'

Shaivism is thought of as one of the oldest, if not the oldest, sect in Hinduism and followers are called Saivas or Saivites. In early Vedic times, an aspect of Shiva was worshipped – Rudra which was associated with wind, storm and the hunt. But Rudra was also the personification of terror and was feared as well as revered by followers. Later, several Upanishads appeared describing Shiva as the highest Supreme Brahman.

Vaishnavism

Also known as Vaisnavism, Vaishnavism is the worship of the Hindu god Vishnu, and the reverence for him is as the original and all-powerful god. He is also known by other names – Naranya, Krishna, Vasudeva, Vithoba and Hari – and the devotional practices that distinguish him from other gods are mainly Bhakti and Bhakti Yoga in which a spiritual and physical discipline must be carried out with an attitude of love and reverence for the divine. These are found in a variety of texts – the Upanishads, the Bhagavad Gita, and the Padma, Vishnu and Bhagavata Puranas.

Vishnu appears in numerous manifestations to preserve and protect the world from evil, chaos and the forces of destruction. He is usually depicted with dark or pale blue skin and with four arms. He holds a lotus flower (*padma*) in the lower of his two left hands; a mace (*Kaumodaki gada*) in his lower right hand; a conch (*Panchajanya shankha*) in his higher left hand; and a discus (*Sudarshana Chakra*) in the higher of his two right hands. In the Bhagavad Gita, Vishnu says, while in the form of Krishna: 'I am the goal, the sustainer, the master, the witness, the abode, the refuge, and the most dear friend. I am the creation and the annihilation, the basis of everything, the resting place and the eternal seed.'

The International Society for Krishna Consciousness, the Hare Krishna movement, has said of Vishnu:

'The largest community within the family of religions called Hinduism worships God under the name of Vishnu ('one who is all-pervading'). Vaishnavas are divided into many smaller divisions, often focusing on one form or avatar (descent) of Vishnu… The two focuses of veneration are Krishna and Rama, who are usually considered God, with other deities in relatively subordinate positions. Vishnavas tend to be personalists, associated with the traditional *bhakti* traditions... From the twelfth century onwards a *bhakti* renaissance swept across India, bringing waves of devotional sentiment. Centres of devotion were rediscovered and revived in places such as Ayodhya and Vrindavana.'

Shaktism

The object of worship for Shaktism is the ancient goddess Shakti who also has the names Devi or Parvati. She is celebrated as the Divine Mother and the 'one without a second'. She is viewed as the creator of the physical universe and as the energy that guides it. The important Shakta scripture, the Devi-Bhagavata Purana says:

'I am Manifest Divinity, Unmanifest Divinity, and Transcendent Divinity. I am Brahma, Vishnu and Shiva, as well as Saraswati, Lakshmi and Parvati. I am the Sun and I am the Stars, and I am also the Moon. I am all animals and birds, and I am the outcast as well, and the thief. I am the low person of dreadful deeds, and the great person of excellent deeds. I am Female, I am Male, and I am Neuter.'

Hindu Texts

The Vedas, Hinduism's oldest scriptures, are considered by Hindus to be *apauruseya* – not of man, but of superhuman creation, written by God. They are described as *shruti*, which means 'what is heard', as opposed to other texts, which are described as *smriti* – 'what is remembered'. The Mahabharata credits the writing of the Vedas to the creator god, Brahma, but the Vedic hymns credit Rishes (sages) after periods of intense meditation. The four Vedas are the Rigveda, the Yajurveda, the Samuveda and the Atharvaveda. Each of these has been split into four major types of text – the Samhitas, the oldest part of the Vedas, which consist of hymns in praise of God; the Aranyakas, dealing with worship and meditation; the Brahmanas, providing commentaries on rituals, sacrifices and ceremonies, to guide priests as they perform their duties; and the Upanishads which discuss meditation, spiritual knowledge and philosophy, the mystical teachings of Hinduism. For some scholars there is a fifth type – the Upsanas, dealing with worship.

The Rigveda Samhita, consisting of 1,028 hymns praising the gods, is the oldest of the Vedas, dating from around 1200 BC. The Yajurveda Samhita is a type of handbook for priests performing the Vedic sacrifices. The Samaveda Samhita presents chants and tunes that can be sung during a sacrifice. The Atharvaveda Samhita, written around 900 BC, consists of pre-Aryan traditions as well as charms and spells.

The Upanishads took their name from the Indian for 'sit down near', as they were taught to students who sat down close to their teachers. Originally in oral form, they provided philosophical knowledge to Hindus and were largely composed between 800 and 200 BC, in both prose and verse, although Upanishads continued to be written until the sixteenth century. Previously, only the *Brahmins* were able to access the knowledge of the universe, but with the Upanishads, it was now available to those believers of high and middle castes who could learn the knowledge from a teacher.

The Bhagavad Gita ('Song of the Lord') can be found in the sixth book of the Mahabharata, composed between 500 and 100 BC. It describes the wars of the house of Bharata, mythical emperor and founder of the Bharata dynasty. A *smriti* text (remembered) it is not perceived to be as important as the *shruti* (heard text) of the Vedas but it remains very important to Hindus. It is a dialogue between Prince Arjuna and his charioteer, Krishna, the prince about to join his brothers in a conflict between two branches of a royal family. In the war, he would be forced to kill many members of his family as well as many friends. Consequently, he does not want to take part, but Krishna teaches him that he has to do his duty and, anyway, he argues, death does not destroy the soul. He adds that knowledge, hard work and devotion lead to salvation and that loyalty to God is the most important thing in life.

Written in 24,000 couplets, the Ramayana, composed at the same time as the Upanishads, recounts the story of Prince Rama who is sent into exile in the forest with his wife, Sita, and his brother Lakshamana. The evil demon, Ravana, kidnaps Sita, but, with the help of the Monkey God, Hanuman, the prince manages to free her, good triumphing over evil.

Hindu Core Beliefs

The Hindu faith is remarkably diverse and there are many beliefs and practices that are not shared by all Hindus. Some core beliefs are, however. Most Hindus would agree, for instance, that the hymns of the Vedas, humankind's oldest religious scriptures, were revealed by the Almighty and that they are the basis of all Hindu belief and practice. It is also agreed that the universe goes through an endless cycle of creation, sustenance and destruction (*samsara*) and that personal destiny is determined by *karma*. To die without your *karma* being resolved, is to face the prospect of being reborn into another body and having to go through the cycle once again. Resolving your *karma* leads to liberation from the cycle of rebirth, or *moksha*.

Most Hindus would agree that it is essential if a believer is to achieve true awakening and *moksha*, he or she needs to work with a teacher who is spiritually awakened – a *satguru* ('true guru'). En route to awakening or enlightenment, meditation, self-assessment, pilgrimage, good moral behaviour, purification and self-discipline are necessary. These are absolute essentials if a believer is to escape the cycle of life and death and attain *moksha*. Worship should be undertaken through personal rituals or as a form of communal devotion, either at home or in a temple. By doing so, communion is achieved with divine beings which live in worlds that humans are unable to see. Most Hindus believe in *ahimsa*. This belief, which can also be found in the Buddhist and Jainist traditions, amounts to respect and reverence for all living things and the avoidance of violence towards others.

Finally, Hindus would subscribe to the notion that there are many religious paths, any of which could lead a believer to awakening and enlightenment, and that there are many manifestations of the divine, but that there is only one Supreme Being of transcendence who is without qualities – beyond description and categorisation; who is omnipresent and who has immanence – meaning that He dwells within each believer.

There is one question that is the subject of considerable debate. Is Hinduism a monotheistic religion? In monotheism, of course, it is believed that there is a single creator God who is almighty, independent, omniscient and omnibenevolent. Hinduism, a divergent network of religious practices, after all, does not really have an answer to this question. And neither does the religion really need an answer to it. Of course, the large pantheon of deities in Hinduism would point to it being a polytheistic religion, but many see the individual gods as forms of the one god, Brahman, which is the highest Universal Principle or the Ultimate Reality in the universe. Hindu worshippers allot devotion to a deity according to their needs at any given time and they are also likely to be complimentary about the deities that other believers make the object of their adoration.

Many contemporary Hindus view each of the various gods simply as manifestations of the Supreme God, championing, therefore, a monotheistic viewpoint – 'monotheistic polytheism' as one source has put it. Matters are confused, however, by the insistence throughout Hinduism's texts that the Divine is everywhere, that Creator and Creation are one and the same thing.

This, therefore, is a question with many answers which is, of course, characteristic of Hinduism as a whole.

Hindu Worship

Worship in Hinduism is usually focused on one or more of the Hindu deities. As might be expected from a religion as diverse as this, worship takes many different forms and is dependent on the community, the location and the language spoken. It is not confined to one place such as a temple although it might take place there and it usually has a purpose, to achieve a specific objective or to enable the person engaging in the worship to break free from the cycle of birth and rebirth.

Upasana is everyday worship. A Hindu might express devotion at home to a *murti* which is an image or statue representing a deity, or *murta*. Veneration of *murtis* is an essential part of achieving the bond of personal love with God and the acts involved are likely to be washing, dressing and garlanding the *murti*. Most Hindu homes have a shrine where offerings of items such as water, flowers, incense and fruit can be made and prayers (*mantras*) can be said. This shrine might be a small room, a small altar or merely pictures or statues of the deity being worshipped. Family members often worship together and rituals should be performed three times daily. Some Hindus like to undertake worship wearing the sacred thread over the left shoulder, hanging down as far as the left hip. This is made of cotton for the *Brahmin* or priest, hemp for the *Kshatriyas* – the ruling or military elite – and wool for the *Vaishyas* or merchants

Hindus worldwide perform a ritual known as *puja* (Sanskrit for reverence, adoration or worship) which is based on the idea of giving a gift or offering to a god, a guest or a distinguished person and receiving their blessing (*ashirbad*) in return. *Aarti* is part of *puja*. Light from wicks soaked in ghee – purified butter – or camphor, is offered to one or more gods. *Aarti* is generally performed by Hindus five times a day, most commonly at the end of a *puja* in South India and at the end of the singing of *bhajan* – songs with religious themes.

In *aarti*, a plate or light is circulated by the priest around a person or a deity, while songs are sung, and the plate or lamp is supposed to acquire the power of the god. Worshippers cup their down-turned hands over the flame and raise their palms to their foreheads, the purifying blessing passing from the image of the god to the worshipper.

The Sanskrit terms *homa* or *yagna* refer to a ritual in which offerings are made to a sacrificial fire, *yagna* being a sacrifice ritual that derives from the practice of Vedic times. The sacrificial fire is the divine *Agni*, the name of Hinduism's fire god. Everything poured into the fire is believed to reach the gods.

There are numerous Hindu festivals throughout the year and around the world. They are often observed with acts of worship, offerings made to deities, fasting, feasting, vigils, fairs, charity-giving and rituals such as *puja* and *aarti*. Typically, a festival will be held in celebration of specific events from Hindu history, often coinciding with the change of the seasons. Some are celebrated by specific sects or in specific regions. The Hindu word for a festival is *Utsava*, meaning, literally, 'the removal of worldly sorrows'.

There is no religious requirement for Hindus to undertake pilgrimages during their lifetime, but they do visit numerous iconic sites of great importance to their religion. The word for pilgrimage is *Tirthayatra* and among places visited are old holy cities such as Puri, Rameswaram and Badrinath. They are part of the *Char Dham* ('Famous Four Pilgrimage Sites'). Major temple cities are visited, places such as Katra, home to the Vaishno Devi Temple and Tirumala, where the Tirumala Venkateswara Temple is located.

Sanskrit

The main liturgical language of Hinduism is Sanskrit, the literary language and spoken language of ancient and medieval India and Nepal. A standardised version of Old Indo-Aryan, Sanskrit originated in the second millennium BC as Vedic Sanskrit but it can be traced back to Proto-Indo-European, spoken from the middle of the fifth millennium BC to the middle of the third millennium BC and Proto-Indo-Iranian, spoken in the late third millennium BC. Sanskrit is the oldest Indo-European language that provides us with written documentation. Its literature includes a wealth of poetry and drama, but there are also scientific, technical, philosophical and religious texts. In the early period, these would have been transmitted orally, having been rigorously memorised, but later they were passed on using variants of the Brahmi script, one of the oldest writing systems, used in South and Central Asia from the first millennium BC. Like Latin in the Roman Catholic Church, Sanskrit is used in Hinduism in hymn and ritual, for instance. Efforts are afoot to restore it as a spoken language and it is classified as an official language of the Indian state of Uttarakhand, as is Hindi. In modern dialect, it is the primary language in a number of villages.

10

Buddhism

'A mind unruffled by the vagaries of fortune, from
sorrow freed, from defilements cleansed, from fear
liberated – this is the greatest blessing.'
Buddha, *Mangala Sutta*

A Religion Outside History

The period in which the Buddha is said to have lived was
five centuries before Jesus Christ, rendering any thought
of historical certitude redundant. With the later figures of
Jesus and Muhammad, we do at least have some kind of real
historical backdrop against which their lives were played
out. But not with the Buddha. It hardly matters, however,
because Buddhism, unlike the other main religions, does not
rely on a deity such as Zeus or Allah. Rather, like Daoism and
Confucianism, it is an ethical religion, championing moral
and ethical principles that can be used to guide a believer to
achieve greater harmony with the universe. It does not rely on
revelations transmitted from God, and there was no moment

of divine intervention in human affairs. Historical accuracy, therefore, has little relevance for Buddhism.

'Buddhism' is a Western name for a religion that practitioners often call the *dharma* which means 'the teaching' or 'the way things are'. For Buddhists, Buddha the man is less important than what he taught. This teaching is said to be able to show people the way things really are which should lead them to rethink their lives. The Buddha's awakening alerted him to this truth and that is what he taught. It is worth noting that he was not the first to achieve enlightenment of this kind; nor was he the last.

The Life of the Buddha

Around five centuries before Christ, a man was born who would, during his own lifetime, become the Buddha ('awakened' or 'enlightened one'). He would renounce his privileged background and the comforts of the world when he reached maturity, would become a seeker of spiritual truth, would undergo a spiritual awakening and become a teacher, travelling, passing on his knowledge and attracting followers.

Most scholars concur that he lived during the era of the Mahajanapadas, the 16 kingdoms that existed in India from the sixth to the fourth century BC. It is believed the ruler of one of these kingdoms at the time, the Magadha Empire, was Bimbisara (r. c. 544-c. 492 BC) and that, when the Buddha finally passed away, Ajatashatru was on the throne. It was the time of the Vedic *Brahmins*, the influential *Sramana* schools of thought and important thinkers such as Mahavira, the 24th *Tirthankara* of Jainism. Buddha was, therefore, one of numerous *Sramana* philosophers alive at that time. Most historians used to date his lifetime to around 563 to 483 BC but in recent times, it is thought more likely that he lived from around 480 to 400 BC. The issue, however, is still open for debate.

He is believed to have been a member of the Shakya clan in the east of the country, the place of his birth perhaps a small republic or an oligarchy of which his father was elected chieftain or oligarch. According to Buddhist tradition, his birthplace was Lumbini in modern-day Nepal and he was brought up in the Shakya capital, Kapilavastu, thought to be in either Tilaurakot in Nepal or Piprahwa in India.

He was born Siddhartha Gautama, into a royal family, his father, Suddhodana, ruling a prosperous feudal realm. On the night the Buddha was conceived, his mother Maya, is said to have dreamt that a white elephant with six tusks entered her right side. As was the custom, she had left Kapilavastu to give birth in her father's kingdom, but Siddhartha was born during the journey, at Lumbini, under a sal tree. Some sources say that Maya, a Koliyan princess, died not long after his birth and he was brought up by his aunt, Maha Pajapati, who was the second wife of his father. He was given the name Siddhartha which means 'he who achieves his aim' and various prophets and seers declared that he would become either a great king or a holy man. When Siddhartha reached the age of 16, his father arranged for him to marry a cousin, Yasodhara, a girl of the same age. The young couple had a son, Rahula, and lived a life of luxury although Buddhist scriptures claim that Siddhartha suffered from doubts about his lifestyle, believing that there was more to life than material wealth.

His father had always tried to shield his son from religion

and from the sickness and suffering of life but, when he was 29, Siddhartha decided to leave his cossetted palace life and go out to meet his father's subjects. He was surprised to see an old man and had to have it explained to him by his charioteer, Channa, that people do, indeed, grow old. On other trips outside the palace walls, Siddhartha also encountered a man suffering from a disease, a dead, decomposing body and an ascetic. Deeply distressed by these experiences, he resolved to try to cure the ailments of life by renouncing his life of privilege and becoming an ascetic.

On his horse Kanthaka, and accompanied by Channa, he clandestinely left the palace for good to become a mendicant, travelling from place to place and relying on donations and the charity of others to survive. He began his new life begging in the street in Rajagaha. King Bimbisara, on hearing what Siddhartha was doing, offered him his throne, but Siddhartha declined the offer, promising, however, that when he had achieved enlightenment, Magadha would be the first place he would visit. Leaving Rajagaha, he studied yogic meditation before moving on to study yoga with Udaka Ramaputta.

By now, he realised that meditation and not extreme asceticism would lead to enlightenment. He discovered the Middle Way or the Noble Eightfold Path, a journey of moderation, denial of self-indulgence, and self-mortification. He would describe this in the *Dhammacakkappavattana Sutta*, a record of the first teaching of Gautama Buddha after he attained enlightenment.

Around this time, he is reported to have accepted rice pudding and milk from a village girl who mistakenly believed him to be a spirit that had granted a wish for her, so emaciated was he in appearance. After this, he sat down beneath a pipal tree which has since become known as the Bodhi tree, in Bodh Gaya. Vowing not to stand up until he had discovered the truth, he waited, in a state of meditation. Meanwhile, those who had been travelling with him – Kaundinya and four others – believed that he had abandoned his search and left him. He is said to have achieved enlightenment after 49 days of meditation. By this time, he was 35 years old and from that moment on, he was known as the Buddha.

It has been suggested that, after his awakening, he was unsure whether it would be worthwhile to try to teach the *dharma* to people, doubting whether they would be able to overcome their ignorance, greed and hatred in order to understand the complexities of the path to enlightenment. In the end, he was convinced, the story goes, by Brahma Sahampati, the most senior of the Mahabrahmas or creator deities who argued that, although many would fail to grasp the necessary principles, some would.

His first lay disciples were two brothers, Taphussa and Bhallika, Afghani merchants who provided him with his first meal after enlightenment. He next travelled to the deer park near Sarnath, northeast of Varanasi in Uttar Pradesh where he first taught the *dharma*. His audience was made up of five other seekers of the truth and with him they created the first *sangha*, community of Buddhist monks. These five became *arhats* ('perfected ones') but in a matter of months, the number of followers of the Buddha had risen to 60. Not long after there were a thousand members of the *sangha*.

For the next 45 years, until his death, the Buddha is said to have taught in Uttar Pradesh, Bihar and southern Nepal, ministering to all classes and types of people, from the elite to servants. The Buddha's father, Suddhodana, constantly sent servants to try to persuade him to return to Kapilavastu, but on each occasion the servants were converted to the *dharma* and joined the *sangha*. Eventually, he did agree to return which led to many members of his family also joining the *sangha*. His son, seven-year-old Rahula, reunited with his father, became one of his ten main disciples. When the Buddha eventually died, Rahula allowed his foster mother to be ordained as a nun, believing that men and women have an equal capacity for enlightenment.

When he was 80 years old, the Buddha announced that he would soon attain *parinirvana*, the state after death that is reached by someone who has achieved *nirvana* during his or her lifetime. With it comes a release from *samsara*. He ate a last meal, a gift from a blacksmith named Cunda and became very ill. He was at pains to ask one of his followers to reassure Cunda that his meal had nothing to do with his sickness and, indeed, it would bring great honour to the blacksmith as it was the last meal consumed by the Buddha.

He died at Kusinara (modern-day Kushinagar), where his last words were reported to be: 'All composite things (*saṅkhāra*) are perishable. Strive for your own liberation with diligence.' The body of the Buddha was cremated and relics were deposited in various stupas and monuments to his memory, some of which are thought to have survived until the present time.

After Buddha

Nothing had ever been written down, and during his lifetime the Buddha's words were passed down orally. The *sangha*, therefore, staged a number of councils in order to reach agreement on Buddhist doctrine and practice. Under the patronage of Ajatashatru, king of Magadha, the First Buddhist Council was chaired by Mahakasyapa, one of the Buddha's principal disciples. Held at Rajgir, probably in 483 BC, possibly just three months after the death of the Buddha, and attended by 500 *arhats*, it attempted to agree on the Buddha's teachings and to regulate monastic discipline.

The Second Buddhist Council took place around 70 years after his death and it brought the first schism in Buddhist ranks. After failing to modify the rules for the Buddhist monastic community, a group of reformers called *Sthaviravadas*, who had wanted to modify the *Vinaya* – the regulations governing the *sangha* – split from the more conservative majority, the *Mahasamghikas*, and created their own sect of Buddhism.

By the time of the Third Buddhist Council in around 250 BC at Asokarama in Pataliputra, when the Emperor Ashoka (r. c. 268-232 BC) of the Mauryan Dynasty was on the throne, the *sangha* needed to be purged of corruption and bogus monks with heretical views. A thousand monks attended. Another three councils were held, the Fourth in the first century BC in Sri Lanka; the Fifth in 1871 in Burma (now Myanmar); the Sixth from 1954 to 1956 in a purpose-built cave at Kaba Aye Pagoda in Yangon in Burma. Generally speaking, these later councils were staged to preserve the teachings and practices of the Buddha as understood in the tradition of Theravada (the branch of Buddhism that uses the Buddha's teaching preserved in the Pali Canon as its doctrinal core).

Buddhism has faced many challenges in the various countries in which it has thrived. Between 836 and 842 BC, the Tibetan emperor persecuted Buddhists in his country and

Chinese officials began to persecute Buddhists in 845 BC. Again in China, in 1949, the Chinese government began a campaign against Tibetan Buddhists that continues to this day.

Branches of Buddhism

Since the death of the Buddha, there has been a constant debate about what really constitutes 'authentic' Buddhism, if, indeed, such a thing exists. Competing schools have argued for the soul of Buddhism for millennia and the argument raged even during the lifetime of the Buddha himself, with disagreements on the basic principles of doctrine and practice.

Buddhism lost its popularity in India as the Muslims began to take hold of the country with their invasions of the eleventh century and it is now very much a minority religion there. However, it spread to Sri Lanka and onwards to Southeast Asia, following the form of the religion known as Theravada. Theravada is still prevalent in Sri Lanka but also in Myanmar, Thailand, Cambodia, Laos and Bangladesh. It means 'Doctrine of the Elders' and its name reflects its scriptural focus on the Pali Canon, the collection of scriptures preserved in the Pali language that is regarded by most scholars as the earliest record of the Buddha's teachings. It was preserved orally and was only committed to writing during the Fourth Buddhist Council in Sri Lanka in around 25 BC, around 454 years after the death of the Buddha.

The Theravada school is the oldest school of Buddhism and, as the principal religion in Sri Lanka and a great deal of Southeast Asia for centuries, has around 150 million followers. It is known for its emphasis on 'sudden awareness'. It also focuses on the objective of achieving the status of the *arhats*, one who has been liberated from the cycle of birth and rebirth.

An opposing school to Theravada is Mahayana which translates as 'Great Vehicle' and which predominates in northern Asia, in China, Mongolia, Korea, Japan and Tibet. The Mahayana school accepts the same scriptures that are used in Theravada Buddhism but it has its own additional devotional and philosophical texts – the Mahayana Sutras. There is also great emphasis on the importance of *bodhisattvas*. These are people who have achieved *nirvana* but insist on continuing to help people still mired in *samsara*. Followers of the Mahayana school call the Buddha Shakyamuni, which translates as 'the enlightened one of the Shakya clan'. For followers of Mahayana, everything already possesses the Buddha-nature; it has only to realise this to arrive at *nirvana*. Mahayana has been good at absorbing and refining local cultures into the way it practises Buddhism and as a result, it can vary according to location.

One of the best known of these variations is that of Zen Buddhism which is popular in China, Japan and Korea, as well as in other parts of the world in recent times. It emphasises direct experience and one's inherent Buddha-nature as opposed to elaborate ritual or the rigorous study of religious scriptures. That is not to say that Zen does not have scriptures and rituals but that they are less important than a relationship with a Zen master and meditation. Zen is one of the most influential and important schools in Buddhism.

Vajrayana Buddhism can also be called Tibetan Buddhism or Diamond Vehicle Buddhism. Believed to have emerged in

India in the sixth or seventh century, more than a thousand years after the demise of the Buddha, its doctrines are said by some to go right back to secret teachings that can be directly attributed to the Buddha. Of course, this controversial claim cannot be proved but it has not prevented Vajrayana Buddhism from becoming very influential. Nowadays, the Vajrayana school is strongly associated with the figure of the Dalai Lama. He is believed by the followers of the Gelug ('Yellow Hat') sect to be just the latest in a long line of figures known as *Avalokitesvara*, believed by devotees to be their repeatedly reincarnated leader whose recurrent rebirth is undertaken in order to bring others to enlightenment. The Dalai Lama has grown to occupy a position of political power in Tibet. This has brought the current Dalai Lama – the fourteenth – into conflict with the government of China which suppresses Tibetan independence as well as any expression of the traditional Tibetan Buddhist religion.

The Paths to Enlightenment

What the Buddha realised beneath the pipal tree can be summed up in the Four Noble Truths – *dukkha*, *samudaya* ('arising', 'coming together'), *nirodha* ('cessation') and *marga* (the path that leads to cessation). All existence, Buddha said, is *dukkha*. It is unsatisfactory and blighted by suffering. We crave and cling to impermanent states and things which means that we are trapped in *samsara*, the cycle of birth and rebirth. The only way to end this is through attaining *nirvana*, ending the craving and, thereby, ending the cycle. This can be accomplished by following the Eightfold Path which is made up of eight different practices: right view – our actions and beliefs have consequences for us after death, as death is not the end; right resolve – the abandonment of home and the acceptance of the mendicant life with the aim of peaceful renunciation; right speech – a life without telling lies or using rude speech and speaking only about the things that lead ultimately to salvation; right conduct – no killing, injuring or taking what is not given and no sexual acts; right livelihood – begging to obtain sustenance and the possession of only that which is necessary to sustain life; right effort – the abstention from sensual thoughts; right mindfulness – the constant awareness of what one is doing and the impermanence of things; and right *samadhi* – the practice of the four stages of meditation (*dhyana*) which results in the unification of the mind.

Nirvana can be attained, the Eightfold Path teaches, by restraint, discipline and the practice of mindfulness and meditation. The Eightfold Path is one of the main teachings of Theravada Buddhism, a path labelled *sila* (morals), *samadhi* (meditation) and *prajna* (insight). Meanwhile, in Mahayana Buddhism it stands in contrast to the *bodhisattva* route, which ends in full Buddhahood. In Samyutta Nikaya ii.124, Buddha says:

'Just this noble eightfold path: right view, right aspiration, right speech, right action, right livelihood, right effort, right mindfulness, right concentration. That is the ancient path, the ancient road, travelled by the Rightly Self-Awakened Ones of former times. I followed that path. Following it, I came to direct knowledge of aging & death, direct knowledge of the origination of aging & death, direct knowledge of the cessation of aging & death, direct knowledge of the path leading to the cessation of aging & death. I followed that path. Following it, I came to direct knowledge of birth… becoming… clinging… craving… feeling… contact… the six sense media… name-&-form… consciousness, direct knowledge of the origination of consciousness, direct knowledge of the cessation of consciousness, direct knowledge of the path leading to the cessation of consciousness. I followed that path.'

Buddhist iconography usually depicts the Eightfold Path as the dharma wheel (*dharmachakra*), a wheel with eight spokes, each of which represents one of the path's eight elements.

The Image of the Buddha

Early in the history of Buddhist art, the Buddha was not himself depicted. He had told his followers to refrain from speculation about his life after his death which may have dissuaded artists from representing him pictorially. He is represented, therefore, by various symbols, the most common of which is the wheel which, as we have seen, is used often to symbolise *dharma*. Around the second century AD, however, figurative depictions began to appear in northern India and the practice of showing him as a human figure quickly spread across Buddhist Asia. The various types of images of the Buddha that we see today illustrate the variety of cultures in which Buddhism has found followers. In fact, Buddhist artists have tried to depict twelve elements of the Buddha's life story, including his previous existence in the Tusita heaven, one of the six deva worlds of the Kamadhatu, located between the Yama heaven and the Nirmanarati heaven. He is said to have resided there as the Bodhisattva Svetaketu before being born on Earth as Gautama Buddha. They also attempt to show his conception; his birth; his education; his marriage and pastimes while still Prince Siddhartha; his renunciation; his asceticism; the Bodhi tree; the defeat of Mara who tried to tempt him with visions of beautiful women; his enlightenment; and his death.

Places of Worship

A stupa is an ancient Indian mound-like structure that contains relics of Buddhist monks or nuns and is used as a place of meditation. Some are believed to actually contain relics of the Buddha himself as these were divided up and placed in a number of locations. His ashes were originally supposed to go back to the Shakya clan of which he was a member but others – six different clans and a king – demanded his relics. To settle the matter, they were divided into ten portions, eight from the relics of the body, one from the ashes of the pyre on which he was cremated and one from the pot used to divide them up. They were enshrined in stupas by the royal families of eight states – Ajatashatru of Maghada; the Licchavis of Vaishali; the Sakyas of Kapilavastu; the Bulis of Allakappa; the Koliyas of Ramagrama; the *Brahmin* of Vethadipa; the Mallas of Pava and the Mallas of Kushinagar. Later, these relics were dug up by the Emperor Ashoka who is said to have divided them into 84,000 portions. Most of these were distributed in stupas across his empire, although some were sent to other countries.

None of the ancient stupas remain intact today but they did become pilgrimage sites and as they gained in prestige, they were made increasingly ornate, often covered in carvings depicting scenes from the life of the Buddha. In Tibet, the stupas evolved into the *chorten*, which has a dome constructed on a five-tier base, symbolising the world's five elements. At the top is a sharp spire with a sun that rests on a crescent moon. This symbolises wisdom and compassion. Meanwhile, in Southeast Asia, the stupa developed into the pagoda, a tiered tower with multiple eaves.

Buddhist Worship

There is a misconception in the West that Buddhist devotion takes the form of monastic contemplation but this is belied by the importance of popular devotion. This began shortly after the Buddha's death, when people would make pilgrimages to stupas containing his relics as a way of gaining merit. At the same time, the places that were important in the Buddha's life – such as Bodh Gaya where he achieved enlightenment – also became popular destinations for Buddhist pilgrims. Others were shown devotion and cults grew up around several celestial Buddhas and *bodhisattvas* such as Amitabha and Avalokiteshvara. Buddha's 18 disciples – the Lohan – also became important in devotional terms.

Buddhist texts were chanted for devotional purposes and the construction of temples began, in which elaborate rituals could be performed. This was encouraged by the fact that it was considered more auspicious to build a new temple than to make good an old one. For Buddhists who are not monks or nuns, devotional acts are extremely important. A favourable rebirth is assured by good actions such as the donation of food to the *sangha*, for instance. Buddhists use ritual in their pursuit of *dharma*. In Buddhism, *puja* are expressions of devotion and worship. These include bowing, the making of offerings and chanting, acts of worship that are usually performed daily at home, either in the morning, in the evening, or both. They may also be performed during communal festivals and on *Uposatha* days – Buddhist days of observance – at a temple.

Meditation (*samadhi*) is of extreme importance. The Eightfold Path names it as its third step on the road to enlightenment. Meditation encourages self-awareness in the practitioner and enables him or her to explore the mind or spirit. The idea of Buddhist meditation was to stop oneself and calm down (*samatha*) combined with *vipasyana*, the practice of seeing clearly within. In this way both mind and body are dealt with and the experience is complete. A spiritual level is attained by ceasing the activities of the day, focusing on something simple and allowing the mind to open and expand. It does not enable the believer to attain *nirvana* but helps him or her along the road to achieving it. *Nirvana* is the ideal destination but it is accepted that meditation helps to make one a better person, leading to understanding, kindness and peace.

Buddhist Texts

Initially, Buddhist texts were passed on orally by the *sangha* and there would have been group recitations at festivals and on special occasions. They were authenticated by the First Buddhist Council in 400 BC and were then memorised and handed down through the generations for centuries. Even today, the tradition of chanting continues, and selected texts are chanted by monks at ceremonies, a sacred act alongside teaching the *dharma*.

The Pali Canon

The Pali Canon is the standard collection of scriptures in Theravada Buddhism and it is preserved in the Pali language, a Prakrit language native to India. The earliest and most complete extant Buddhist canon, it was first written down at the Fourth Buddhist Council which took place around 25 BC in Sri Lanka. It was transcribed in three sections – Vinaya Pitaka, Sutta Pitaka and Abidhamma Pitaka and is known as the Triptaka which means 'three baskets'.

The Vinaya Pitaka is made up of the 227 rules of conduct and discipline that apply to the lives of Buddhist monks and nuns. In its turn, it is divided into three parts and in addition to the rules themselves, it explains the circumstances when a rule is applied and provides exceptions to that rule.

The Sutta Pitaka contains the main teaching or *dharma* and is divided into five *Nikayas* ('collections'). These are the long teachings (*Digha Nikaya*); the medium length teachings (*Majjhima Nikaya*); shorter teachings that are grouped according to their subject matter (*Samyutta Nikayan*); and a collection that is arranged according to the subjects discussed (*Anguttara Nikaya*); and shorter verse and prose texts.

The Abidhamma Pitaka is a philosophical analysis of the teaching, probably written by monks and made up of seven books that are termed the higher or further teaching. As with the others, the monks wrote on dried palm leaves that had been cut into rectangles and etched with a metal stylus that was rubbed over with carbon ink. The pages were held together by a thread that was passed through them and their covers were beautifully painted pieces of wood.

The Sanskrit Canon

The Buddha supported the notion of teaching appropriately, according to the students who were listening, and instructed the *sangha*, therefore, to teach in the languages of those they were teaching. In India it took the form of oral Sanskrit and at the first-century BC Fourth Council, the oral teachings were written down in in Sanskrit, becoming known as the Sanskrit Canon. As with the Pali Canon, it can be traced back directly to the teachings of the Buddha. The Sanskrit Canon was also, like the Pali Canon, split into three sections: the Vinaya Vaibasha – rules for the monastic life; the Sutra Vaibasha – the *dharma* and the five Agamas of which it was made up were exactly like the five Nikayas of the Pali version; and the Abidharma Vaibasha – scholarly analysis.

Mahayana Texts

As Mahayana Buddhism increased in popularity, new Sutras were written and the teaching to be found in the Sanskrit Canon was merged with Mahayana teaching. The new Sutras incorporated new material embodying Mahayana ideas. Amongst these are: the Prajnaparamita Sutras (Wisdom, Perfection Sutra), which set out the teachings of Emptiness (*Sunyata*); the Saddharma Pundarika Sutra (the Lotus Sutra), praising the Buddha and explaining the oneness of his teachings. In Mahayana Buddhism, this was considered the supreme teaching, and it is the most important Sutra to Chinese and Japanese Buddhists; the Vimalakirti Nirdesa Sutra explains that a layperson can become a *bodhisattva*; and the Sukhavati Sutra teaches that Amitabha's celestial realm was open to all believers, Amitabha being a celestial Buddha in Mahayana Buddhism.

Chinese, Japanese and Korean Texts

Buddhism arrived in China in the first century AD and the Sanskrit texts were translated into Chinese from around 200 AD until about 1200 AD. This was done in the beginning by non-Chinese monks but the work was taken over by Chinese monks, state translation initiatives were established and original Chinese Sutras were added. The Chinese Tripitaka was created with the Chinese Sutras added to it. Multiple copies of the Sutras could be made following the Chinese invention of wood-block printing in the eighth century and, in fact, the oldest book in existence is the Diamond Sutra which was printed in 868 AD. In the tenth century, the Tripitaka was printed in Korean and the Chinese version was taken to Japan and copied, being published in the seventh century.

11

Jainism

'Righteousness consists in complete self-absorption
and in giving up all kinds of passions including
attachment. It is the only means of transcending the
mundane existence. The Jinas have said so.'
Vardhamana Mahavira

Tirthankaras

Jainism is another religion with its origins in India. The
name is derived from the Sanskrit word *'Jina'* which means
'conqueror' and *Jinas* – as Jain *arihants* are called – are also
known as *Tirthankaras* (which means 'builders of the ford
across the ocean of rebirth'). The *Jinas* or *Tirthankaras* are
religious teachers who, like *bodhisattvas* in Buddhism, have
achieved enlightenment, having overcome *samsara*, the
eternal cycle of birth and rebirth. The teachings of these
men have absolute and indisputable authority and provide
followers with a means to cross over from *samsara* to spiritual
liberation.

Jainism split early in its history into two main sects. Digambara is more popular in South India, while Shvetambara is dominant in the northwest of the subcontinent. It is thought that they split after the Council of Valabhi at Saurashtra in the fifth century. At this important conference, the Shvetambara Canon was established and agreed upon but no one of the Digambara persuasion had been invited, leading to their displeasure. Although Jainism today has numerous branches, they are generally associated with either Shvetambara or Digambara.

There are between four and five million Jains, mostly living in India although there are communities in Canada, Europe, Kenya, the United Kingdom, Hong Kong, Suriname, Fiji and the United States.

Vardhamana Mahavira and the origins of Jainism

Vardhamana Mahavira (582 or 599-510 or 527 BC) was the 24th *Tirthankara* of Jainism. He is often perceived as the founder of the religion, but that would be wrong as, of course, there were 23 *Tirthankaras* before him. He was born at Kundagrama in modern-day Bihar in Northeast India, not far from the modern city of Patna. His father was King Siddhartha and his mother Queen Trishala, both members of the Ikshvaku dynasty. Lord Rama from the Ramayana is from this dynasty, as are 21 of the 24 *Tirthankaras*. The Digambara texts claim Mahavira was born in 582 BC, while the Shvetambara texts hold that the year of his birth was actually 599 BC. According to the 'Universal History' of

Jain mythology, he had undergone numerous rebirths before his sixth-century birth. These are said to have included him living as a hell-being, a lion and, just before his birth as the 24th *Tirthankara*, it is suggested he had been a *deva* (god). Shortly after his birth, he is said to have been visited by the god Indra who is said to have anointed him and performed his *abhisheka* – consecration – on the sacred, mythological Mount Meru.

Mahavira grew up a prince but, at the age of 30, renounced the privileges of royal life, leaving his family and the palace to lead an ascetic life, the hardships he suffered described in the Acharanga Sutra. He lived this way for twelve and a half years before attaining the state of *Kevala Jnana* (omniscience, supreme knowledge) at the age of 43. It is said to have occurred under a Sala tree on the banks of the River Rijupalika near Jrimbhikagrama. He took his knowledge to others and began to teach, travelling across India for the next 30 years, according to the Shvetambara. The Digambara maintain that he remained in his *Samavasarana* (preaching hall), teaching followers who came to him.

He is said to have started out with eleven disciples, known as the *Ghandharas*, the head of whom was Gautama. These men memorised and orally transmitted Mahavira's teachings after his death. Jain tradition says that Mahavira had 14,000 *muni* (male ascetics), 36,000 *aryika* (nuns), 159,000 *sravakas* (laymen), and 318,000 *sravikas* (laywomen) as his followers. Amongst them were King Srenika, popularly known as Bimbisara, of Magadha, Kunika of Anga (r. c. 492-c. 460 BC or c. 565-535 BC) and Chetaka of Videha (fl. 5th century) whose sister was Mahavira's mother.

Mahavira died at the age of 72, in Pawapuri in Bihar, and

his *jiva* (soul) is believed by all Jain traditions to have gone to *Siddhasila*, the abode of liberated souls. It is said that his main disciple Gautama attained *Kevala Jnana* on the night that Mahavira died. There are various accounts of the leader's death, some saying that he had a simple death, while others describe a death in which he was surrounded by gods and kings. One account says that he preached for the last time for six days to a large crowd of followers. Everyone fell asleep and when they awakened, he had vanished, leaving behind only his nails and hair which were cremated by his disciples. His life of spiritual teaching and his awakening are remembered at *Diwali*, the same night on which Hindus celebrate their festival of lights.

According to Jain tradition, the teachings of Mahavira were gradually lost around 300 BC when the monks looking after them were dispersed by a famine that ravaged the Magadha region. The monks made efforts to reassemble the canon once more but differences between their recitations and Mahavira's teachings were evident. In the fifth century AD, efforts to deal with these variations were unsuccessful and the two Jainist traditions, Shvetambara and Digambara, continued to use their own incomplete and different versions of Mahavira's teachings.

The two Jainist factions disagreed about monastic practice. The Digambaras insisted that an ascetic who had truly given up the world would also relinquish the need for clothing and go naked, as Mahavira had apparently done. The Shvetambaras disagreed, however, maintaining that his teachings did not make nakedness an absolute prerequisite. They believed that wearing simple white garments was sufficient. This dispute gave the two factions their names –

Shvetambara means 'white-clad' while Digambara means 'sky-clad'. Their disagreements are not just about attire (or the lack of it). There are also scriptural differences, disputes about the rules of monastic life and about the life of Mahavira as well as a fundamental argument over the status of women. Shvetambaras are happy to admit women to full monastic vows, but Digambaras refuse to do this, insisting that women are not capable of achieving *Kevala Jnana*. Only when they are reborn as males is it possible and, therefore, only men are admitted to the monastic life. This opposition was exacerbated during the early years of Jainism by the fact that the two groups not only held such different views but were also located in different areas of India with different cultures, the Digambaras in the south and centre of the country, the Shvetambara in the north and west.

Despite these internal rifts, the Jains had grown into a powerful entity by the fifth century AD. The Digambaras won royal patronage in central and southern India and became important in cultural matters such as the development of vernacular literature. A couple of centuries later, the Shvetambaras enjoyed similar status in the north, but they were particularly influential in the west of the subcontinent.

Jainism spread into diverse areas and grew in membership, but by the eleventh and twelfth centuries, as Hinduism began to take hold, the two Jainist factions began to decline in influence and power, retreating into the geographical areas where they are today concentrated. The Shvetambaras were also squeezed by the growth of Islam in the north from the twelfth century onwards. By 1500, Jainism arrived at the point at which it still finds itself. Its geographic spread would not change over the next 500 years but this did not prevent various efforts to reform it and renew its appeal to Indians. The Shvetambaras had a prominent movement called *Sthanakavasi* which remains active to this day. Its members are recognisable by the fact that they wear cloths or masks over their faces. They reject the worship of images which led to the majority of Jains, who do venerate images, being known as *Murtipujakas*, or 'image-worshippers'.

Jainist Belief

There is no deity in Jainism, and the actions and behaviour of an individual determine his or her position in the cycle of rebirth. Self-denial is a major feature. By practising that, followers hope to achieve *moksha*, the release from the constant suffering of the cycle of rebirth. Monks and nuns swear the Five Great Vows which are non-violence (*ahimsa*); being truthful (*satya*); celibacy (*brahmacharya*); not stealing another's property through action, speech or thought (*asteya*); and non-possessiveness (*aparigraha*). Of greatest importance is *ahimsa* which means non-violence not only towards human beings but to all creatures, including the tiniest organisms.

The Five Great Vows are reserved for Jain monks and nuns but lay Jains swear lesser vows that cover similar subjects. Jains are strictly vegetarian enforced by the vow not to harm any creature. Some even refuse to cut flowers and will only use those that have fallen from the plant in their rituals. They follow the path of the Three Jewels (*Ratnatraya*) – the right faith (*Samyak Darshana*); right knowledge (*Samyak Gyana*); and right conduct (*Samyak Charitra*). Observance of these leads to the liberation of the soul, it is believed. A Fourth

Jewel is sometimes mentioned – right penance and atonement for sins.

Confession of sins is at the heart of the annual *Samvatsari* festival. Eight days of fasting and abstinence during the monsoon season is followed by the confession of the sins of the past year to family and friends while followers swear not to carry grudges into the coming year. On a daily basis, Jainists give over one-thirtieth of a day – 48 minutes or a *Muhurta* – to meditation. Followers receive special merit by donating food to monks and nuns and are expected to serve others, engage in religious study, refrain from passion and be polite and humble at all times. Adherence to such behaviours helps to reduce *karma*.

There are stages to be gone through in order to achieve liberation. Fourteen of these are noted in the ancient Jain text, the Tattvartha Sutra, written sometime between the second and the fifth centuries AD. The first stage is *Mithyadrishti* in which the soul does not believe in the right path to salvation; the fourteenth – *Ayoga Kevali* – is the point at which the soul leaves the body and attains liberation. This last stage is beyond the reach of ordinary believers and is open only to monastic Jains.

Places of Worship

Jains worship in temples or they may have shrines in their own homes, the temple perceived to be a replica of the celestial halls in which the *Tirthankaras* continue to teach. Worship and contemplation of images of the *Tirthankaras* help the believers on their road to spiritual enlightenment.

Darshan, as in Buddhism, is eye contact with the image of the *Tirthankara* while reciting a mantra. In Jainism, the most important mantra is the *Namokara* mantra which is the first prayer that a Jain follower will utter when meditating. Reciting this, the Jain will bow to the *Panch Parameshti* (Supreme Five). These are *Arihant* – those who have defeated the four karmas; *Siddha* – liberated souls; *Acharyas* – spiritual leaders; *Upadhyaya* – teacher of less advanced ascetics; and *Sadhu* – monks or sages. The prayer is not directed at a particular god, but towards the *guna* which is the good qualities of the gods, teachers and saints. It is a prayer that does not seek anything; it merely pays respect to teachers and those who are spiritually evolved and it reminds devotees that their ultimate goal is *moksha*.

12

Sikhism

'Even kings and emperors with heaps of wealth
and vast dominion cannot compare with an ant filled
with the love of God.'
Guru Nanak

The Founding of Sikhism

Founded in the fifteenth century in India's Punjab region, Sikhism is a monotheistic religion that currently has around 30 million followers, making it the fifth largest religion in the world. Although founded in the subcontinent, its practitioners may now be found in many other parts of the world but more than 90 per cent of Sikhs live in India and they represent 2 per cent of India's population. However, large Sikh communities can be found in the United Kingdom, the United States and in Canada. In India, Sikhs are generally to be found in the north-western and northern states and, in the Punjab, they amount to 58 per cent of the population.

The word 'Sikh' is derived from the Punjabi verb *sikhna*

which means to learn. Originally to be a 'sikh' meant to be a 'follower' or 'disciple' but, as the Sikh movement developed through the centuries into a fully-fledged religion, it came to be defined more precisely. Indeed, according to the Sikh Code of Conduct, the *Rahit Maryada*, a Sikh is:

'any person who believes in God; in the ten Gurus; in the Guru Granth Sahib and other writings of the Gurus, and their teaching; in the Khalsa initiation ceremony; and who does not believe in the doctrinal system of any other religion.'

The founder and principal driver of Sikhism in its early years was Guru Nanak who was born into a Hindu family on 15 April 1469 in Talwandi in the Punjab. The city, now known as Nankana Sahib in tribute to him, was situated 80 kilometres to the west of the present-day Pakistani city of Lahore. He was a precocious child, to say the least, more intelligent than his teachers, apparently, and questioning of Hindu and Muslim religious practices. He refused, for instance, to wear the sacred garments customarily worn by Hindus, preferring a faith that was inward rather than the divine protection of a physical object. He was greatly supported by his older sister, Bibi Nanki, who became his first follower. Her important role in the life of her brother was an example of the gender equality that has become a central tenet of the Sikh religion.

Nanak married and had two children, working at a government-owned granary in Sultanpur but meditating each day on a riverbank before going to work. At the age of 30, he disappeared for three days, and a search had to be mounted for him. When he finally returned, he announced:

'There is neither Hindu, nor Muslim, so whose path shall I follow? I shall follow God's path. God is neither Hindu nor Muslim and the path I follow is God's.'

His account of the revelation is recalled by him in the *Adi Granth*, the Sikh scriptures:

'I was a minstrel out of work.
I became attached to divine service.
The Almighty One commissioned me,
"Night and day sing my praise".

The master summoned the minstrel
To the High Court, and robed me with the clothes of honour, and singing God's praises. Since then God's Name has become the comfort of my life.

Those who at the Guru's bidding feast and take their fill of the food which God gives, enjoy peace. Your minstrel spreads your glory by singing your Word. By praising God, Nanak has found the perfect One.'

He spent the ensuing 20 years travelling widely on journeys that are called *Udasi*, persuading men and women that they should follow what he called God's path. The destinations of each of these journeys are still subject to debate but they are traditionally said to have taken him in each of the four cardinal directions – east, west, north and south, across the subcontinent and modern-day Pakistan, Tibet and the countries of Arabia. His fifth and final *Udasi* was a journey around his own home state of Punjab. His companion on these journeys was a Muslim minstrel from his home village,

Bhai Mardana, who would become a significant character in the Sikh religion. He was presented in the scriptures as a man filled with doubts and the Guru explained to him the meaning and point of his message.

On his travels, there were two key themes he was promulgating. Firstly, Naam Japna which involves singing hymns or contemplating the qualities of God. Secondly, he advocated following awakened individuals who were known as *Gurmukh*. This, he reasoned, was better than sticking to selfish motives and self-absorption, known as *Manmukh* which only leads to frustration and danger.

Around 1520, his journeys completed, he returned to Punjab, living in Kartarpur, northeast of Lahore, on the banks of the River Ravi for the rest of his life. There, he continued to teach, but also worked in the fields, earning a living.

Sikhism After Guru Nanak

Guru Nanak died, aged 70, on 22 September 1539, but before he passed away he had selected the new Guru to lead his followers. Bhai Lena (1504-1552) took the name Guru Angad, meaning 'part of you'. Like Guru Nanak, Guru Angad had been a Hindu and had, in fact, first heard Nanak when he was on a Hindu pilgrimage. As Guru, his principal achievements included the formalising of the Gurmukhi alphabet from Indo-European scripts. This was used to write the Sikh scriptures. He also collected the hymns of Nanak, contributing 63 of his own hymns to the Sikh canon. He strove to eliminate illiteracy, launching schools for this purpose and helped to establish Sikhism as a real religion that would be practised for centuries to come. Guru Angad died in 1552, but as his predecessor had done, he selected his successor before he died.

Guru Amar Das (1479-1574) was already 70 years old when he became Guru but he grew the Sikh religion during his tenure. He championed the equality of Sikh women as well as *Langar*, the Sikh tradition by which anyone, regardless of social status, would be given free food. Importantly, he also introduced the *Manji* system of appointing trained clergy, a system that continues to operate to this day.

Guru Amar Das appointed his son-in-law, Jetha Ram Das (1534-81) as Guru before he passed away, an appointment badly received by Guru Amar Das's sons. They forced Ram Das to relocate to an area where he founded the town of Ramdaspur that would develop into Amritsar, now the holiest city of the Sikhs. He enhanced the *Manji* system for appointing clerics and formalised other areas of the religion, especially the daily rituals that Sikhs were expected to practise. Unlike the previous Gurus, he appointed one of his sons – Guru Arjan (1563-1606) – as his successor and, in fact, the next six Gurus were all his direct descendants. This appointment created splits in the Sikh community but Guru Arjan commissioned a *Gurdwara* – the names Sikhs give to their places of worship – which would become the Golden Temple, the Sikh religion's holiest place, in the middle of Amritsar. He also instigated agricultural projects for poor farmers and composed several thousand hymns that became part of Sikh scripture.

As these acts gave the Sikh religion a higher public profile, they also brought dangers for it. The new Mughal emperor, Jahangir (r. 1605-27) looked upon this growth of Sikhism with a great deal of suspicion, viewing it as a threat to his empire and to his own religion, Islam. In 1606, after Guru Arjan refused to remove references to Hinduism and Islam from Sikh scriptures, and after he supported Jahangir's rebellious son, Khusrau Mirza (1587-1622), Jahangir had Guru Arjan arrested, tortured and executed. The Sikh religion had its first martyr.

Guru Arjan's successor and sixth Guru, was his son, Guru Hargobind (1595-1644). He became Guru when aged just 11, but as he grew older sought to avenge his father's death by making Sikhism a militaristic organisation. This was symbolised by the fact that he always wore two swords that represented *miri* and *piri* – temporal power and spiritual authority, respectively. He ordered the construction in front of the Golden Temple of the Akal Takht ('the throne of the timeless one') where justice could be administered and temporal matters discussed. It is the highest seat of earthly authority of the Sikhs' Khalsa – their collective body. Guru Hargobind was the Sikh leader during a difficult time and was in power for more than 37 years, longer than any other of the ten Gurus.

The next three Gurus were Har Rai (1630-61), Har Krishnan (1656-64) and Tegh Bahadur (1621-75). The tenth Guru, Gobind Singh, was a very significant figure in Punjabi history, founding the Khalsa Panth, the Sikh army, to fight the Mughals and ensure that Sikhs could always defend themselves. The defeat of the Mughals was not accomplished until after his assassination in 1708 by two Afghans on the orders of the Muslim army commander, Wazir Khan (1635-1710). Before he died, however, he changed the nature of his religion forever, issuing a decree that named the scripture of

Guru Arjan Dev – the *Adi Granth Sahib* – as the eleventh and final Guru of Sikhism. Gobind Singh's successor was not human.

The Mughal Empire fell to a number of separatist movements, amongst which were the Sikhs, in 1739 and 30 years later, the Sikhs saw off an Afghan invasion army and became a significant political force in the Punjab. In 1800, the Sikh leader, Ranjit Singh (r. 1792-1801), established the Sikh Empire across northern India, although his government was secular. Religions of all persuasions were tolerated in the new empire. The Sikh Empire fought against the British in two Anglo-Sikh Wars, the first from 1845 to 1846 and the second from 1848 to 1849. They were defeated and became the last part of India to be annexed by the British Empire. The Sikh Empire was no more.

Following partition of India in 1947, there were hopes for an independent Sikh nation, but the idea was doomed to failure. In the months leading up to partition there was a great deal of violence between Sikhs and Muslims and on partition, thousands of Sikhs migrated over the border into India. Tensions remain between Sikhs and Muslims in the Punjab to this day.

Sikh Beliefs

Having emerged as a direct response to Hinduism and Islam, Sikhism inevitably borrows from each of those rival religions. It also rejected elements of each, such as the array of deities followed by Hindus. Instead, Sikhism accepts only one eternal God who created the universe and is without form but present in all things. Human beings can never, to their minds, completely understand God, a belief that concurs with the Muslim view. Sikhs differ from Muslims, however, in believing in reincarnation in which a being gathers truth over a number of lifetimes and the goal of all humans should be to attain total understanding and truth. When that happens, the human being is one with God and the cycle of birth and death ceases.

Sikh leaders were called Guru, a word derived from the Hindu faith and the ten Gurus of history serve as guides on the passage to eternal truth, along with the Sikh holy scripture, the Guru Granth Sahib, which was named as the eleventh and last Guru, as we have seen.

The most important precepts of Sikhism are the concepts of *Simran* and *Sewa*. *Simran* is derived from the Sanskrit word *smarana* which means 'act of remembrance, reminiscence and recollection'. It is the continuous contemplation of the finest parts of the self and of God. *Sewa* is a service to others which is undertaken with no expectation of any reward for its performance. This may be large or small and can take the form of formalised practices or individual giving or helping. Through these two ideas, spiritual salvation can be achieved.

Distractions from the right path come in the form of five evils, as explained by the Gurus. These are lust (*Kam*), rage (*Krodh*), greed (*Lobh*), attachment (*Moh*) and ego (*Ahankar*). Sikhs are expected to be aware of these dangers at all times and to reject them. There are also five virtues that help Sikhs on the path to God and truth. These are truth (*Sat*), compassion (*Daya*), contentment (*Santokh*), humility (*Nimrata*) and love (*Pyare*).

Equality is important to Sikhs and this includes all human

beings, no matter their religion or ethnicity. This even extends to everybody being able to use Sikh community facilities and services. Women are treated as equal to men and are able to participate in and even lead in worship.

Sikhs are encouraged to stand up to injustice. This is found in the concept of *Sant Sipahi* ('saint-soldier'). This idea demands strict discipline in both mind and body. A *Sant Sipahi* will defend and protect the innocent physically and spiritually but not necessarily with the use of physical force. That, the tenth Guru Gobind Singh said, is 'a last resort when all other peaceful means have failed.'

Sikh Practice and Ritual

The first Guru, Guru Nanak, introduced the Three Pillars of Sikhism that are the cornerstone of the Sikh religion. Firstly, *Naam Japna* is meditation, the singing of hymns from the Guru Granth Sahib, meditating upon the names of God, particularly the chanting of the word *Waheguru* ('Wonderful Lord'). Secondly, *Kirat Karni* is the leading of an honest and pure life, using what God has provided – skills, talents and abilities – to help both oneself, one's family and society in general. The final Pillar of Sikhism is *Vand Chakna*. This is sharing what you have – food, wealth and other things within your community.

In order to become a member of the Khalsa, the Sikh community, an individual must first be ritually baptised. Both men and women may be baptised and, following the ritual, Sikhs – both men and women – must wear the five Sikh articles of faith, known as the five Ks. These are the *kesh*

– a knife or sword; the *kangha* – a small wooden comb that is used twice a day and is worn in the hair at all times; the *kara* – an iron bracelet; the *kachera* – a special type of cotton undergarment; and the *kirpan* – a dagger that is a symbol of the Sikh's duty to come to the defence of those in peril.

A baptised Sikh man is identified by the turban he must wear to cover his long, uncut hair. This distinctive headgear symbolises, for Sikhs, piety and courage and is wound round the head. Women may also wear the turban.

Religions of the East

13

China

'What you do not want done to yourself,
do not do to others.'
Confucius

The Shang

Chinese religion developed without any influence from
the other great world religions, mainly because of China's
isolation from the rest of the world. It is distinctively different,
therefore, to religions found elsewhere. God, for instance,
plays no part in Confucianism which has sometimes meant
that it has not been considered a religion at all. Nonetheless,
it *is* a religion and was the main religion of China for a very
long time.

Chinese religion of the distant past is an unknown quantity
to us. The second historical dynasty of the country was the
Shang which followed the Xia and lasted from 1766 to 1122
BC. Although we have little detail of it, religion seems to
have been important to the Shang, and their lives were greatly

influenced by spirits and mystical powers who had to be appeased by sacrifice. Records exist of the complex techniques of divination practised by the Shang. They used 'oracle bones' to ask questions of the spirits and recorded the answers on a turtle-shell or on an ox's shoulder-blade.

Interestingly, some of the Shang religious notions were carried on long after their dynasty had faded into history, especially the belief in the balance of nature which became the well-known concepts of *yin* and *yang*. Also a constant in Chinese religion is the emphasis on the well-being of people, an idea that developed through time into *t'ien-ming* – the Mandate of Heaven – the Chinese political and religious doctrine that was used to justify the rule of the Emperor of China. It meant that, if a ruler was overthrown, he had lost the Mandate of Heaven, heaven's permission to rule. Natural disasters and famines were also perceived as indications that the Mandate of Heaven had been withdrawn from the ruler of the time.

Confucianism

Confucius

Confucianism developed out of the thinking of the Chinese philosopher, Confucius (551 BC-479 BC), as he is known in the West (born Kong Qiu). Not much is known about him, but it is thought he was born into a fairly well-off family in the area of Zou which is close to present-day Qufu in northeast China. His father died when he was three years old and he was brought up by his mother. Aged 19, he married Qiguan and the couple had three children together. He was educated at an ordinary school and is said to have worked in several civil service roles in his early twenties and as a bookkeeper. He also looked after sheep and horses, saving enough to provide a proper burial for his mother, who died when he was 23. He was appointed governor of a town in the state of Lu in eastern China, and rose to the position of Minister of Crime in the state government.

Anxious to spread his philosophy and his political thoughts, Confucius set out on a series of journeys, visiting the courts of numerous Chinese states but failing to have his philosophy implemented. At the age of 68, he returned home and spent his remaining years teaching his disciples. He edited the *Book of Songs* – an anthology of ritual hymns, heroic verses and pastoral odes – the *Book of Documents* and other ancient classics including the *Spring and Autumn Annals*, the court chronicle of Lu. Han dynasty historian Sima Qian (c. 145 or 135 BC-86 BC) reports that 'In his later years, Confucius delighted in the *Yi*', or *I Ching*, the divination manual that is still popular both in the East and the West to this day. These works began to be described as 'Confucian Classics' and the perception grew of Confucius as the spiritual ancestor of later Chinese teachers, philosophers, historians and literary scholars.

Confucius died at the age of either 71 or 72 and was buried in the Kong Lin cemetery in Shandong Province.

Confucian Thought

The teaching of Confucius was gathered by his disciples in the *Analects*, a collection of his sayings that demonstrate how much disdain he felt for the disorder and instability of the time in which he lived. Of paramount importance to him were the Mandate of Heaven and ancestor worship which, he believed, represented the best of Chinese history. He was mainly interested, however, in social relations and the proper conduct of human affairs, concerned that people recognised their responsibility to others and developed a doctrine of benevolence, the notion of *ren* or love for one another. He defined this in sayings such as: 'What you do not wish for yourself, do not do to others.' Asked by a student to define *ren*, Confucius replied: 'One should see nothing improper, hear nothing improper, say nothing improper, do nothing improper.' He emphasised individual responsibility, that we are all responsible for our own actions and that, even though we have no influence over how long we are alive, we are the only ones who can determine what we achieve during our time on earth.

He championed strict rules of behaviour, particularly the behaviour of inferiors to superiors. Naturally, he believed that the subject should always obey the ruler who, as the Son of Heaven, should obey heaven. In family affairs, too, he emphasised a strict hierarchy – a son should obey his father, a younger brother should obey his older brother and a wife should obey her husband.

Indeed, women did not fare well in his teachings. Marriage was not about love. Rather, it was an arrangement and its objective was to prolong the family and the family name. The *Book of Songs* makes clear the attitude towards women:

Sons shall be born to him –
They will be put to sleep on couches;
They will be clothed in robes

Daughters shall be born to him –
They will be put to sleep on the ground
They will be clothed in wrappers

Ritual and etiquette – *li* – were provided for every occasion. Although these seem like pointless formalities to the modern eye, they were actually very useful at a time when social structures were under threat and respect for authority was declining. Confucius was particularly interested in the correct behaviour of a gentleman – *junzi* – and even describes what was proper attire for such a man:

'A gentleman does not wear facings of purple or mauve, nor in undress does he use pink or purple. In hot weather he wears an unlined gown of fine thread loosely woven, but puts on an outside garment before going out of doors. With a black robe he wears black lambskin; with a robe of undyed silk, fawn. With a yellow robe, fox fur. On his undress robe the fur cuffs are long; but the right is shorter than the left. His bedclothes must be half as long again as a man's height… Apart from his court apron, all his skirts are wider at the bottom than at the waist.'

Confucius established a decorous way to behave, providing, for instance, instructions to bow twice when seeing a messenger off. He went as far as to describe how a *junzi* should lie in bed, avoiding the posture of a corpse. These instructions were *de rigueur* for many generations of Chinese functionaries.

He insisted that the gentleman accepts his place in the social hierarchy and does his utmost to perform according to this role rather than attempt to better his position. 'The superior man,' he said, 'does what is proper to the station in which he is; he does not desire to go beyond this.' Even rulers did not escape his strictures. He exhorted them to be cognisant of the welfare of the people over whom they ruled. They should never be taken for granted, he reminded them, or exploited in any way. He maintained that good government created happiness and promoted order and stability. He wrote:

'Govern the people by regulations. Keep order among them by chastisements and they will flee from you, and lose all self-respect. Govern them by moral force, keep order among them by ritual and they will keep their self-respect and come to you of their own accord.'

In effect, a good and humane ruler was defined by his attitude to *ren*. To lose his focus on this might mean forfeiture of the Mandate of Heaven and a fall from power. Of course, if a ruler followed the road advocated by Confucius, he was forced to surround himself with functionaries who also adhered to Confucian notions of how a *junzi* should behave. In 136 BC, therefore, during the Han dynasty, competitive examinations based on Confucian ideals were introduced for the imperial civil service. By the time of the Song dynasty – 960-1279 AD – it was believed by the Chinese that even heaven had taken on board the thinking of Confucius and was thought to be an exact reflection of the court on earth. The deities themselves were a kind of heavenly civil service.

But, of course, God and heaven were not the source of Confucian principles. He believed they existed in the hearts and minds of people and it could be said that his religion was humanistic, more akin to moral philosophy than religion. But it was perhaps his reverence for ancestors and his insistence on the rites and ceremonies that paid tribute to them that helped his system to be perceived as a religion. This perception was helped during the Song dynasty by the scholar Zhu Xi (1130-1200) who introduced elements of Daoism and Buddhism to Confucianism, creating what has come to be known as Neo-Confucianism.

Emperors recognised the value of Confucianism in maintaining order and stability and, therefore, keeping them in power and, consequently, Confucianism became the state religion of China. It maintained this position and influence on Chinese life throughout the twentieth century, although during the Cultural Revolution of the mid-1970s, it was criticised for being too socially conservative. In post-Mao China, a form of Confucianism called New Confucianism has developed. It champions the concept of Harmonious Society, a response to perceived social injustice and inequality in China.

Daoism

Laozi

Nature and harmony run through Chinese religious thought and the origins of Daoism are rooted in it. The *Daode jing* ('The Way and Its Power'), the first and most important text of Daoism, is said to have been written by the Chinese philosopher Laozi (*fl.* 6th-5th century BC). There is some doubt as to whether Laozi actually existed. Traditionally he is depicted as a sixth-century contemporary of Confucius, but some modern historians place him in the fifth or fourth century BC. He is said to have been a court archivist for emperors of the Zhou dynasty and earned the name Laozi, which means 'the Old Master' because of the wise counsel he provided. Although he is traditionally believed to have written the *Daode jing*, its authorship is disputed. The oldest part certainly dates back to the fourth century BC, but modern scholars consider other parts to have been written, or compiled, much later.

Legend has it that Laozi eventually disappeared, a disappearance that remains a mystery. It is said that, having recognised that the Zhou dynasty was in decline, he left the court and headed west, looking for a place where he could enjoy solitude. A border guard recognised him and asked if he could give him a token of his wisdom. Laozi proceeded to write the *Daode jing*, which he gave to him. He then resumed his journey and nothing was ever heard of him again.

The *Daode jing* recognises the *dao* or 'Way' as the power or principle that exists in everything and that maintains the order of the universe. In order to ensure cosmic harmony, one should search out this *dao*. By so doing, the follower will achieve spiritual advancement and will lead a happier, more virtuous and even longer life. In order to follow the *dao*, it is necessary to distance oneself from material things and eschew disruptive emotions such as anger and ambition. A peaceful, simple life is the way to the *dao*, and one should act in a manner that is harmonious with nature rather than act for the benefit of oneself. The *dao* is eternal and never changes. Rather it is life that is in turmoil around it. One should employ the concept of *wu wei* ('non-action'), defined by one sinologist as an 'attitude of genuine non-action, motivated by a lack of desire to participate in human affairs'. In the *Daode jing*, Laozi emphasised actions and behaviours that encouraged *wu wei* such as humility, non-interference, submissiveness and detachment from the material world.

Daoism seeks the kind of balance that Laozi found in contemplating the nature of the universe and in the Chinese concept of *yin* and *yang*. *Yin* is everything that is dark, soft, cold, moist and feminine while *yang* is associated with light, hard, warm, dry and masculine. By maintaining a balance of the two, harmony can be attained, according to Laozi. It can be achieved in Daoism through meditation, and *tai chi*, the internal Chinese martial art that promotes mental, physical and spiritual exercise to balance the *qi*, the life-force in the body. *Tai chi* is now hugely popular in the West, as well as China.

During the Han dynasty (206 BC – 220 BC), Daoism became a religion, its meditation techniques believed to lead the practitioner to eternal life. But, it has to be said that immortality was not intended to be taken literally when discussed by Laozi in the *Daode jing*. This did not stop those who treated Daoism as a religion from reassuring themselves that by seeking *dao*, they could actually attain immortality.

14

Japan

Shinto

'The gods of Shinto are the life of the natural world in
all its rich variety. The sacred does not lie outside of
life but is one with it.'
James Heisig, American philosopher

Early History of Shinto

Shinto is the traditional religion of Japan. It is essentially
devotion to invisible spiritual beings and powers – *kami* –
shrines and various rituals. The most important factor is not
to be able to explain the world, as many religions try to do,
but to communicate with the *kami*. These are spiritual beings
that are concerned with human beings. They are grateful for
our interest in them and they want us to be happy. Treated
well, they are able to intervene in our lives and bring us good
things – health, success in business or in exams. In fact,
Shinto does not separate the natural physical world and the

spiritual world. Similarly, there is no division between body and spirit. Spirits, such as *kami*, inhabit the same world as we do and everything, to practitioners, is merely part of one unified creation. People who are followers of Shinto practice and ritual, can also be followers of other belief systems, such as Buddhism. It is not exclusive.

In its early days, long before the arrival of Buddhism in China in the sixth century AD, Shinto was not a formal, organised religion. Instead, there were many local beliefs, stories and practices. These would later be brought together and called Shinto. Prehistoric peoples in Japan seem to have adopted animist practices, worshipping natural spirits, found in such things as plants, rocks and trees and natural phenomena, such as earthquakes and storms, those same spirits that today are called *kami*. This resulted in a great and complex tradition of folklore in Japan and early Japanese history was filled with the rituals and stories about these spirits. In reality, these practices and beliefs can be considered to be precursors to Shinto. These early Japanese people developed such rituals and stories to provide them with a spiritual and cultural world that allowed them to create the story of their origin and give shape to the world they lived in, making sense of it.

The Arrival of Buddhism

The arrival of Buddhism in the sixth century AD brought change to the early Shinto faith and the traditions that had developed around it. It began to adopt elements of Buddhist thought and practice and, later, when Confucianism emerged, it, too, wielded influence over the old beliefs. In fact, a number of shrines that had been used for Shinto worship, were converted into Buddhist temples or Shinto shrines existed inside Buddhist temples with Buddhist priests supervising them. It was obviously advantageous for the ruling elite to use the three religions – Shinto, Buddhism and Confucianism – to retain control over their subjects and the government became deeply involved in religion with the establishment of the government ministry, the Department for the Affairs of the Deities.

Shinto was a far simpler belief system than its two rival religions which led to them being treated as intellectually superior. As Japanese theology and philosophy developed people were drawn more to the rich complexity of Buddhism and Confucianism. Buddhism began to grow into a powerful force and even took on a political role as the Japanese centralised government strengthened its grip on the country.

As *kami* were important to the life of an individual, so they were equally important to the welfare of the nation and this meant that the emperor had the duty of performing meticulous ceremonies and rituals in order to assure the nation of prosperity and peace. These ceremonies incorporated elements of Buddhism and Confucianism and became an official part of the government's administrative calendar. It remained thus until comparatively recently. In the seventh and eighth centuries, the divine status of the emperor, as the descendant of the sun goddess Amaterasu, became embedded in Japanese culture and shrines to the royal family were created.

Religion played a large role in Japanese government

between the eleventh and fifteenth centuries. In the sixteenth century, Christian missionaries began arriving in Japan but, viewed by the government as a political threat, they were dealt with ruthlessly. Buddhism, albeit with a Shinto influence, became dominant in the seventeenth century, a time when the government forced every Japanese person to register at a Buddhist temple. They also had to pay to be a Buddhist. The state took over the running of the temples and the training of Buddhist priests.

Gradually, a purer form of Shinto was emerging, a Shinto that told the Japanese people that they were the descendants of gods and that they were a superior race. Extraneous Buddhist elements were removed and Shinto began to coalesce as a belief system.

The Meiji Restoration

In 1868, the religious situation in Japan changed dramatically as did the nation's politics. The name of the so-called Meiji Restoration derives from the emperor who brought it about – Meiji (r. 1867-1912). Practical imperial rule was restored and the political system was reorganised under his leadership. Shinto underwent a complete transformation. It was separated from Buddhism and all elements of Buddhism were removed from Shinto shrines. Buddhist deities were demoted and the priests lost their positions, replaced by Shinto priests. Shinto now became part of the government administration. The goddess Amaterasu, who had been treated as a fairly minor god, was now elevated to high status as a deity and was employed to validate the emperor's position as the high priest of Shinto which became the state religion. It was championed by military leaders, with the emphasis firmly on the divine status of the emperor. Shinto's devotion to *kami*, ancestor worship and loyalty to the family and to the emperor and the nation, was now a unifying force in Japanese society, culture and politics.

Because of its deep connection with Japanese culture and society, Shinto was declared 'non-religious'. It had somehow become Japan, a representation, as one historian put it, of 'the cultural will or energy of the Japanese people, embodied in conventions that precede or transcend religion'.

Shinto Today

When Japan was defeated in the Second World War, the emperor – Hirohito (r. 1926-89) – was forced to explicitly reject the claim that he was an *arahitogami* – an incarnate divinity. From being an 'imperial sovereign', he became a 'constitutional monarch', forced to write:

'The ties between us and our people have always stood on mutual trust and affection. They do not depend upon mere legends and myths. They are not predicated on the false conception that the Emperor is divine, and that the Japanese people are superior to other races and fated to rule the world.'

Shinto was viewed as being inextricably associated with the expansionist military government that had so disastrously taken Japan to war. The Americans were particularly hostile to the religion, perceiving it to be a cult run by the government, a religion that had been turned into a militaristic and nationalistic ideology to inspire Japanese soldiers in the war. The new constitution introduced in Japan after the war made sure that religion and state were kept totally separate. Article 20 of that constitution states:

1. 'Freedom of religion is guaranteed to all. No religious organisation shall receive any privileges from the state, nor exercise any political authority.
2. No person shall be compelled to take part in any religious acts, celebration, rite or practice.
3. The state and its organs shall refrain from religious education or any other religious activity.'

Shinto is still very important in Japan, despite being divested of its focus in the emperor and being no longer the centre of administrative life. Elements of Shinto belief are still maintained – reverence for the natural world, ancestor worship and the maintenance of shrines. These are observed even by people who are not devout followers of the religion. There are still festivals and, despite the best efforts of the Americans, some imperial ceremonies that have an air of Shinto mysticism about them.

Shinto Beliefs and Practices

Shinto worship involves a great deal of meticulously observed ritual which can be undertaken in the home or at shrines and which, although it was formalised when the religion was under government control in the nineteenth century, still enjoys a degree of local variation. Shinto ceremonies are designed to satisfy aesthetically as well as spiritually and they are also intended to be pleasing to the *kami* for whom the worship is being undertaken. Worship may be private or enjoyed in the company of others. An individual may pray to specific *kami* in order to obtain a desired situation or object or to give thanks to the *kami* for something pleasing that has occurred.

Often a Japanese home will have a space dedicated to a shrine. It is called a *kami-dana* (*kami* shelf) and here offerings are made of food or flowers, for example, and prayers may be said. The shelf is positioned high on a wall and contains items associated with Shinto ceremonies. The most important is the *shintai* which is meant to house the *kami* that is the object of the worship. *Kamidana shintai* are more often than not small mirrors, but they can also sometimes be stones, jewels or other objects.

The object of most Shinto rituals is to guard against evil or to seek something. Sins may also be cleansed, not only to gain personal peace but also to ensure that devotees are pure enough to approach the *kami*. The purification rituals that begin all ceremonies and rituals are known as *harae* and water and salt are used. The ritual typically performed before entering a shrine is *Misogi*. Water is used in this. *Kagura* is an ancient ritual dance that used to involve possession by the *kami* while *Ema* are small wooden written signs or plaques that can be used for written prayers. Blessings form part of other rituals.

The ceremonies held before the construction of a building, office or house are called *jichinsai*. They are aimed at purifying the ground on which the building will stand, pleasing the local *kami* and ensuring safety during the actual build. During ceremonies, ritual prayers – *norito* – are incanted to the *kami* by a priest on behalf of the worshippers. These are uttered in formal Japanese phrases of great beauty and, in fact, Shinto holds that there are specific words and phrases which, if spoken correctly, possess spiritual power.

Shinto Texts

Shinto has several important holy books. The *Kojiki* ('Records of Ancient Matters'), commissioned by the Empress Gemmei (r. 707-715), are collections of ancient myths and traditional teachings that had, until then, been passed down orally from generation to generation. The myths cover the origins of the four islands of Japan and of the *kami*. They serve a political purpose as well as a cultural one, insisting on the supremacy of Japan and the Japanese over all other countries and races. They also confirm the status of the ruling elite and emphasise the political superiority of the Yamato clan over the Izumo. The myths explain how the *kami* share many human qualities; they are different from God in the way he is viewed in the West; they have a duty to take care of humanity; humanity has a duty to look after the *kami*; if humanity is to survive, purity and purification are essential and purification is an act of creativity as well as of cleansing; and death is the ultimate impurity.

The *Rikkokushi* ('Six National Histories') detail the mythology and history of Japan from the earliest times until 887 AD. The sources were official records archived at the Japanese Ministry of Central Imperial Affairs as well as the biographies of officials held at the Ministry of Ceremonial Affairs. This collection contains a number of different texts. The *Nihon Shoki* ('Chronicle of Japan'), also known as *Nihongi*, are 30 books, taking in the mythological period up to 697 AD; the *Shoku Nihongi* ('Chronicle of Japan, Continued'), also called *Shokki*, are 40 volumes that cover the period from 697 to 791; the *Nihon Koki* ('Later Chronicle of Japan') are 40 volumes that cover the years from 792 to 833; the *Shoku Nihon Koki* ('Later Chronicle of Japan, Continued') consists of 20 volumes that detail the period from 833 to 850; the *Nihon Montoku Tenno Jitsuroku* ('Veritable Record of Emperor Montoku of Japan'), also known as *Montoku Jitsuroku*, are 10 books covering 850 to 858; and the *Nihon Sandai Jitsuroku* ('Veritable Record of Three Generations [of Emperors] of Japan'), also known as *Sandai Jitsuroku* which are 50 volumes covering from 858 until 887.

Abrahamic Religions

15

Judaism

'Hear, O Israel: The LORD our God, the LORD is one.
Love the LORD your God with all your heart and with all
your soul and with all your strength. These commandments
that I give you today are to be upon your hearts. Impress
them on your children. Talk about them when you sit at
home and when you walk along the road, when you lie
down and when you get up.'
Deuteronomy 6:4-7

Abraham, Isaac and Jacob:
The Founding of Judaism

Judaism is one of the oldest surviving religions. It developed
out of the beliefs of the people of Canaan in the southern
Levant and is the first recorded monotheistic religion in
history. The history of the Jews goes back to at least around
1500 BC and Judaism is said to have first developed with the
prophet Abraham, who promulgated the notion of one God in
the Middle East. Abraham first appears in the Bible as Abram,

in the eleventh chapter of the book of Genesis, working as a shepherd, in what is now called Iraq. It was a time when polytheism was predominant but Abram rejects that, insisting that there is just one true God. God tells him to abandon his homeland and go and settle in Canaan which was situated roughly where modern-day Israel, the Palestinian territories, Lebanon and west Jordan are located today. Abram has been promised three things if he agrees to move – he will be close to God; he will be blessed with numerous descendants, despite the great age of him and his wife; and he will have a new land, as explained in Genesis 12:1-3:

'I will make you into a great nation,
  and I will bless you;
I will make your name great,
  and you will be a blessing.
I will bless those who bless you,
  and whoever curses you I will curse;
and all peoples on earth
  will be blessed through you.'

Abram does have children; the first – Ishmael – with an Egyptian handmaid named Hagar and another with his wife, Sarah. He becomes known as Abraham, the 'Father of Many Nations' but God puts him through a series of trials, the most severe of which is a command to sacrifice his son Isaac. He is about to comply with God's command when he is interrupted by an angel who prevents him from going through with it. His obedience of God's will has been successfully tested, and he is given a ram to sacrifice instead. Thus, did Abraham, his son Isaac and Isaac's son Jacob become known as the Patriarchs of the Jewish faith, the founders of the religion. The terms Jewish and Judaism had not been established at this point, but the three Patriarchs are recognised by Jews as being part of their religious tradition. Jacob's name becomes Israel and his twelve sons continue with the monotheistic tradition of their father, grandfather and great-grandfather, founding the Twelve Tribes of Israel.

When Canaan is ravaged by famine, Jacob and his sons relocate to Egypt where their descendants become slaves. A number of generations later, Moses is appointed by God to lead his people out of slavery and back to their homeland of Canaan. This became known as the Exodus and during it the Israelites face many trials and experience many miracles. These include God attacking them with plagues and the Nile being turned to blood. When they are threatened by the Egyptian army that is pursuing them, God commands Moses to hold out his staff over the water of the Red Sea and during the night, a strong wind divides the water, allowing the Israelites to cross. The water returns as the Egyptians try to follow and the army is destroyed.

At Mount Sinai, God speaks to Moses once again, renewing His covenant with the Israelites. God promises that they will be His 'treasured possession' if they observe the Ten Commandments given to Moses on stone tablets inscribed by God. When the Israelites begin to worship a golden calf, however, a false god, Moses becomes angry and breaks the tablets. God remakes the tablets and they are placed in a case called the Ark of the Covenant that is carried by the Israelites to Canaan.

Although there are Ten Commandments on the tablets, God gives Moses many more commandments and the Torah, the Jewish holy scripture, lists some 613. These regulate daily life, property disputes, explain how to deal with cases of murder and theft and so on. They stipulate what Israelites should eat, who they can marry and detail sacrificial rites that are to be performed by hereditary priests. They are the rules for the just governance of a society.

Meanwhile, Moses dies before the Israelites reach the promised land of Canaan, but first addresses the Israelites, reminding them of the covenant they have with God and how God will bless them if they adhere to the commandments.

Judaism in Antiquity

The Hebrew Bible details the establishment of the United Monarchy of Israel and Judah under the leadership of Saul, dated traditionally as between 1050 and 930 BC, the capital of which was Jerusalem. After the reign of King Solomon (r. c. 970-931 BC), however, the kingdom split in two. In the late eighth century BC, the Kingdom of Israel was captured by the Assyrian King Sargon II (r. 722-705 BC). Meanwhile, the Kingdom of Judah remained independent until its capture by the Babylonians in the early sixth century BC. During the Siege of Jerusalem in 587 BC, the Babylonian army destroyed Solomon's Temple, also known as the First Temple, which was the centrepiece of Jewish worship at the time. Judah's ruling elite was taken to Babylonia, returning to their homeland 70 years later. This period is known as the Babylonian Captivity and is viewed as the first Jewish diaspora. Meanwhile, a Second Temple was constructed in 516 BC on the Temple Mount in Jerusalem. It would stand until 70 AD and was host to the Great Assembly, a Jewish council that was headed by the priest Ezra. Around this time the final few books of the Old Testament were written.

A form of Judaism that blended the Jewish religious tradition with elements of Greek culture emerged around the third century AD. Hellenic Judaism would be centred on Alexandria in Egypt and Antioch in modern-day southern Turkey. The arrival of the Romans prompted rebellions by the Jews against Roman rule. After the Great Revolt (66-73 AD), the Second Temple was destroyed by the Romans. Jews were persecuted, study of the *Torah*, and celebration of Jewish holidays and circumcision were proscribed. Almost all the Jews of Judah were removed from the kingdom. In 200 AD, however, Jews were permitted to become Roman citizens. Judaism was recognised as a legitimate religion of the Roman Empire.

Judaism from the Middle Ages to Modern Times

In the Middle Ages, Jews living under Muslim rule were generally treated fairly. They enjoyed tolerance of their beliefs and were allowed to integrate. Expulsions and massacres did take place, however, through the centuries. But, in Europe, Christian suspicion of Jews and the belief held by many Christians that the Jews were responsible for the death of Jesus Christ, led to persecution, pogroms, forced conversions, massacres, expulsions and the establishment of ghettos in which Jewish people were forced to live in unsatisfactory conditions. The First Crusade (1096) brought the destruction of Jewish communities on the Rhine and the Danube and, in the Second Crusade of 1147, French Jews were put to the sword. The ensuing Crusades brought more deaths and expulsions.

In the thirteenth, fourteenth and fifteenth centuries Jews were banished from England, France and Austria respectively. They were blamed for the Black Death that killed millions of Europeans in the middle of the fourteenth century and many Jewish communities were destroyed.

Of course, the persecution of Jews reached its horrific apogee during the period of Nazi rule in Germany and during the Second World War. Approximately 6 million Jews were exterminated in what the Nazis described as 'The Final Solution', the genocide of European Jews in death camps and in the gas chambers. Following the war, in 1948, the state of Israel was established in the Middle East with its capital at Jerusalem. There was an influx of Holocaust survivors and Jews from Arab and Muslim countries. Israel lives uneasily with its Arab neighbours to this day.

The Covenant

The laws presented in the Torah are considered by Jews to be binding, of course, but many, such as those concerning sacrificial rites, either no longer apply or are inappropriate. Thus, there are a range of interpretations of these commandments. Nonetheless, traditional Jewish people observe the Sabbath and they observe the various Jewish religious festivals and celebrations. Dietary laws, such as not eating pork, are also upheld. For Jews to eat the meat of an animal, it must chew its cud and have split hooves. Although pigs have split hooves, they do not chew their cud. In the same way, Jews should only eat fish that have both fins and scales. These instructions can be found in the Bible in Deuteronomy, Chapter 14:8-10:

'And the pig, because it has a split hoof, but does not chew the cud; it is unclean for you. You shall neither eat of their flesh nor touch their carcass.

These you may eat of all that are in the waters; all that have fins and scales, you may eat.

But whatever does not have fins and scales, you shall not eat; it is unclean for you.'

The covenant with Abraham promised the land of Canaan to the Israelites but, as the Bible reminds us, it was given only on condition that they observed the commandments. Eventually, they were conquered by their enemies and exiled. It must be remembered, however, that the promise of the land was eternal. Therefore, if they did lose it, they still could maintain the hope of returning there.

Jewish Beliefs

It is not easy to define what Jewish people believe, for the religion has no group of core precepts on which everyone agrees. They certainly agree on the question of monotheism and certain scriptures are accepted by just about everyone, but there are no required beliefs. Rather, there is required behaviour. This makes sense when one considers that the Jewish faith is concerned with the relationship between humankind and God, between Israel and the rest of the world and between individuals. There is, of course, formal belief, but it is a faith that is about doing, about action. The Golden Rule is a moral principle that can be found also in the other great faiths and it is important also to Jews. As one famous rabbi put it: 'Do not do to your neighbour what you yourself hate. That is the Torah, and all the rest is commentary. Now go study.'

In Judaism, it is believed that we are all, both Jews and non-Jews, *b'tzelem Elohim*. In other words, we are all made in the image of God. We are all as important as one another and we have the potential to do good in the world. Therefore, what matters are the choices we make in life and the consequences of those choices.

The 13 Principles

As has already been noted, Judaism does not have a formulated set of beliefs that all branches of the faith recognise and, unlike Roman Catholicism, for instance, there is no central authority. Authority is derived, rather, from the sacred writings, laws and traditions of Judaism.

Perhaps the closest thing to such a central statement of the tenets to which Judaism holds can be found in the 13 Principles of Faith created by Rabbi Moses ben Maimon (1135 or 38 -1204) who is perhaps better known as Maimonides or Rambam. He was the greatest medieval Jewish philosopher and the principles he cited were believed to be the minimum beliefs to which a Jew should adhere. They were: God exists; God is one and unique; God is not a physical being; God is the first and the last – eternal; He is the only god to whom prayer should be directed; the words of the prophets are all true; the prophecy of Moses is true and he is the greatest of all the prophets; the Torah was given to Moses; there will be no other Torah; God knows all our deeds and thoughts; God punishes those who break the commandments and rewards those who obey them; the Messiah is coming; and the dead will rise.

Rambam's principles appeared in his commentary on the *Mishnah*, otherwise known as the 'Old Torah', the first major work of Rabbinic literature. At the time, Jewish theologians were trying to come up with such a list. They were controversial when they were first promulgated and, indeed, were largely ignored by Jews for the next few centuries. Eventually, however, they grew in importance and became the most widely accepted statement of Jewish belief.

Jewish Life

People can become Jewish through conversion, but a Jew is defined, according to Orthodox Jewish law, as one who has been born of a Jewish mother. Jewish boys are circumcised when they are eight days old, a religious ritual performed by a *mohel*, a Jew who is trained in the practice of *brit milah* (circumcision). At this point the child is given a Hebrew name.

The boy is schooled in the Jewish religion by his mother and, from the age of five, he takes lessons in religion at the synagogue after school. On the *Shabbat* after his thirteenth birthday, a Jewish boy becomes *Bar-Mitzvah* ('son of the commandment' or 'son of the law'). The boy reads from the *Torah* in the synagogue for the first time and this is usually followed by a party attended by family and friends. Following this, he will be expected to carry out all the duties and responsibilities of a Jewish man. A Jewish girl becomes a *Bat Mitzvah* ('daughter of the commandment' or 'daughter of the law') at the age of 12. Nowadays it is usual to hold a ceremony to mark this event.

A devout Jew prays three times daily: in the morning, in

the afternoon and in the evening. This may be undertaken either at home or at the synagogue. A Jewish man has to cover his head when praying, a hat or a skull cap (*yarmelka* or *kippah*) being worn for this purpose. The prayer shawl, the *tallit*, is worn at morning prayers. It is tasselled or fringed at each of its four corners, as stipulated by the *Torah*. He may also on weekdays wear phylacteries (*tephillin*) – black boxes made of leather strapped to the forehead and upper arm, that contain four passages of scripture: Exodus 13:1-10 and 11-16; Deuteronomy 6:4-9 and 11:13-21. The head covering may continue to be worn as a sign of respect for God.

Food eaten in a Jewish home should be *kosher* – clean or pure. Care must be taken not to serve meat and dairy products at the same meal and two different sets of dishes are used for each type of product to prevent confusion. This also means two washing-up bowls and two tea towels for each set of implements and crockery. The types of meat that Jews can eat are stipulated in Leviticus 11 and Deuteronomy 14.

Jewish Festivals

The most important day of the Jewish week is the *Shabbat*, a celebration both of the creation of the world and the Exodus – the escape from Egypt of the people of Israel. It begins at sunset on Friday evening with the lighting and the blessing of the *Shabbat* candles by the mother of the household and ends with the appearance of three stars in the sky on Saturday night. The man of the house, often accompanied by their children, will go to the synagogue. On his return home, before dinner he blesses his wife and children, using the words of Chapter 31 of the Book of Proverbs. Verses 10 to 31 are called *Eshet Hayil* and are in praise of a good wife or the 'ideal woman' of Judaism. A special loaf called *challah* is eaten. Jews are not permitted to undertake any work on the *Shabbat* and there can be no fires unless they are lit before sunset on Friday. Moreover, no long journeys may be made. Orthodox Jews may not drive or take public transport on the *Shabbat*. They have to hope, therefore, that their synagogue is close to home. After a restful day, the family gathers for blessings (the *Kiddush*) over wine and sweet spices.

The 'pilgrim' festivals are important to Jews – the eight-day festival of *Pesach* (Passover), *Shavuot* (Pentecost) and *Sukkot* (Tabernacles). *Shavuot* celebrates the gift of the *Torah* by God to Moses. It also signifies the bringing of the first fruits back at the time when the Temple still stood. *Sukkot* commemorates God's protection of the Jewish people during the Exodus and *Pesach* celebrates the freedom of the Jews after being enslaved in Egypt. *Rosh Hashanah* is a New Year festival, the culmination of 40 days of penitence, with special food, prayer and a service the next day during which the *shofar* – a ram's horn – is regularly blown, symbolising a 'wake-up call'.

The Day of Atonement is called *Yom Kippur* and is the holiest day of the year for Jews. It is observed with around 25 hours of fasting and prayer and most of the day is spent at services in the synagogue.

The Torah

The Hebrew word 'Torah' means 'instruction' or 'teaching'. It refers in Judaism to the first five chapters of the Jewish

Bible and is the most important scripture for those of the Jewish faith, also known as *Torah Moshe* (the Law of Moses). These chapters are the first five books of Moses, known in Hebrew as *Hamishah Humsei' Torah* – *Bresheit* (Genesis); *Shemot* (Exodus); *Vayicra* (Leviticus); *Bamidbar* ((Numbers); and *Devarim* (Deuteronomy). The *Torah*, Jews believe, was given to Moses on Mount Sinai after the Jews fled captivity in Egypt and they believe that it shows Jewish people how they should live and behave. The book contains, as we have already noted, the 613 commandments and ten of these are known to Jews as the Ten Statements of the Decalogue. The *Torah* is, of course, written in Hebrew. The word *Torah* is also used in a wider sense, referring to the written and oral law of Judaism, thus encompassing all Jewish scripture.

In a synagogue, the *Torah* scrolls are kept in an ark – *Aron ha kodesh* – an ornamental closet or receptacle. They are taken out of the ark three times a week. Small sections are read on Mondays and Thursdays and the morning of *Shabbat* (Sabbath) brings the main reading. The scroll will be read in sequence during the year until it has all been read. The start-point for this is the autumn festival of *Sukkot*. The reader has to be very practised in this as the letters are written without vowels. Therefore, the reader has to already have a very good understanding of the section he is reading, and the reading is sung and not just spoken.

When the scrolls are unrolled on the *Bimah* – the raised platform that is located in the centre of the synagogue – they must not be directly handled. Instead a kind of pointer (*Yad*) is used. The chanting of the words is normally undertaken by a rabbi, but occasionally a member of the congregation is invited to perform the task which is a great honour known as an *Aliyah* ('going up').

It can take 18 months to make and handwrite a *Torah*. It is done by a *sofer* ('scribe') and the parchment is made from the skin of a kosher animal, usually a cow. Accuracy is essential and a single error can lead to the whole scroll being rendered invalid. When it is finished, it is called a *Sefer Torah*, *sefer* being the Hebrew word for book. *Torahs* are greatly valued by their communities and if one is dropped by accident in the synagogue, the congregation must fast for 40 days as punishment. In times of persecution, Jews have gone to great lengths to preserve their holy books.

There is also spoken or oral Jewish law – the *Torah she b'al pei* ('*Torah* from the mouth'). These are the laws that are not recorded in the Five Books of Moses, or 'Written *Torah*'. They incorporate a variety of rituals, worship practices, dietary laws, statements about relationships, both interpersonal and between man and God, festival observance, marriage, agriculture and civil claims. The Oral *Torah* was passed down from generation to generation but was finally written down after the Second Temple – on Temple Mount in Jerusalem – was destroyed in 70 AD and Jewish culture was seriously threatened.

Other Jewish Scriptures

Tanakh

Also known as the *Mikra* or the Hebrew Bible, the *Tanakh* is the authoritative collection of Jewish texts. It is also a textual source for the Old Testament of Christianity. There are some passages written in Biblical Aramaic, but it is mainly written in Biblical Hebrew. This Hebrew text is known as the Masoretic Text. Composed of 24 books, the *Tanakh*'s name is an acronym, employing the first letter of each of the Masoretic Texts' three subdivisions – *Torah*, *Nevim* ('Prophets') and *Ketuvim* ('Writings'). It is unclear when the Hebrew Bible canon was established. Some say that it was during the Hasmonean dynasty, the dynasty that ruled Judea and surrounding regions between 140 BC and 37 BC; others claim that it was compiled in the second century AD or later. The *Talmud* says that it was compiled by the men of the *Anshei K'nesset HaGedolah* (the Great Assembly), and was completed by 450 BC.

Mishnah

In the *Mishnah* can be found the *halakhot*. These are the regulations that govern everyday daily Jewish life and deal with ritual purity. The first major work of Rabbinical literature, it was compiled by Rabbi Judah Ha-Nasi (c. 135-219 AD) around the beginning of the third century AD, put together at a time when Jews were suffering persecution and there was a fear that some of the oral traditions would be lost or forgotten. Jews who upheld the strictures of the *Mishnah* would be showing commitment to the *Torah*. They would, therefore, be guarded in turn by the *Torah*. The *Mishnah* was of extreme importance to the Jews who were dispersed around the world but parts of it came very quickly to be considered difficult or obscure and to remedy this a companion volume was compiled that was easier to use.

The *Mishnah* is divided into six parts – *Zera'im* (Seeds) which deals with laws on agriculture, prayer and tithes; *Mo'ed* (Festival) which deals with the Sabbath and the holy festivals; *Nashim* (Women) which is about marriage, divorce and contracts; *Nezikin* (Damages) dealing with civil and criminal law, the functioning of the courts and laws on oaths; *Kodashim* (Holy Things), which is about sacrifice and laws for the Temple and the diet; and *Tohorot* (Purities) dealing with ritual purity and impurity.

Talmud

Talmud translates from the Hebrew as 'learning' or 'instruction' and is the comprehensive written version of Jewish oral law, as well as all the commentaries on it that followed. Compiled in the second century AD, it is the source for the Jewish code of law – *Halakha* – and consists of the *Mishnah* and the *Gemara* which is made up of rabbinical analysis of and commentary on the *Mishnah*. The rabbinic debates on the *Mishnah* took place between the second and fifth centuries AD in Jerusalem and, later, in Babylon. The Babylonian version holds more authority.

As part of their worship, some Jews consider it their duty to study one page of the *Talmud* every day. Known as *Daf Yomi* (Hebrew for 'page of the day'), this practice began after the First International Congress of the World Agudath Yisrael World Movement in 1923.

Jewish Mysticism – Kabbalah

Mysticism is taken very seriously by Judaism, in that it represents a way of experiencing things other than purely through the senses. The Kabbalah is a set of esoteric teachings that sets out to explain the relationship between *Ein Sof* – infinity – and the earthly and finite universe that was created by God. It is not a religion. Rather, it is a mystical religious interpretation of the nature of the universe, the human being, and the nature of existence, and it also asks a number of other fundamental questions. This Jewish mystical tradition originated in Spain, although it can be said to relate to many other traditions. In fact, various schools of Jewish esotericism have emerged at different times during Jewish history, often reflecting mystic traditions of the past but also dovetailing with their own cultural and social milieus.

The main scripture of the Kabbalah is the *Zohar* which, although it is attributed to Simeon bar Yohai (*fl.* 70 AD), was actually first published in Spain in the thirteenth century by a Jewish writer named Moses de Léon. Following the expulsion of the Jews from Spain in 1492, the Kabbalah first became known in the West, and a school of Christian Kabbalists emerged. With the Jews' expulsion, Safed in Galilee became the centre for Jewish mysticism and it was there that Rabbi Isaac Luria (1534-1572) reinterpreted the Kabbalah.

Kabbalah tries to define the nature of the universe and humanity, why we are here and other philosophical questions. Through an understanding of such matters, spiritual realisation can be achieved.

Judaism Today

Today, there are estimated to be around 13 million Jews in the world. Naturally, the largest number is to be found in the United States which is home to 5,700,000 people of the

Jewish faith. This, however, amounts to just 2.1 per cent of the American population. Israel is home to 5 million Jews, which is almost 78 per cent of the country's entire population. The knowledge and expertise of Jewish people have gained them eminence in many fields, including entertainment, law and politics which is all the more impressive when one considers the catastrophic loss of Jewish lives at the hands of the Nazis between 1933 and 1945. Of course, Israel has been the hub of Jewish life since its founding in 1948. Jews from around the world – from more than 100 different cultures – have come to live on this tiny piece of land that, in places, is no more than 12 miles wide.

There are currently many different schools of thought within Judaism. Reform Judaism developed in the late eighteenth century, during the Enlightenment, the intellectual and philosophical movement that championed ideals such as liberty, progress, tolerance and constitutional government. Laws that prohibited Jewish interaction with the rest of the world were reduced, permitting Jews to gain access to secular education and greater experience of the world outside Judaism. In Central and Western Europe there was a Jewish response to this, known as *Haskalah* – the 'Jewish Enlightenment'. Also around this time, in Central Europe, Great Britain and the United States, *Erform* (also known as Liberal) Judaism emerged. This relaxed many of the laws and conventions that had isolated Jews. In reaction to Reform Judaism, Modern Orthodox Judaism developed, the instigators claiming that Jews could operate in modern life while still adhering to Jewish law. The Conservative Movement came about after rich Reform Jews in the United States funded Orthodox European Jewish scholars, who were critical in their study of the *Talmud* and the Bible, in the establishment of a seminary that trained rabbis for immigrants from Eastern Europe. They were joined by right-wing Reform rabbis who insisted that Jewish law should still be maintained. Meanwhile, Orthodox Jews who did not support the *Haskalah* founded Haredi Orthodox Judaism. As can be seen from all of this, there are many forms of Orthodox Judaism.

Reconstructionist Judaism was based on the ideas of the Jewish scholar, Mordecai Kaplan (1881-1983). It saw Judaism as a progressively evolving civilisation. It has greatly influenced Judaism and has led many to reassess fundamental elements of the Jewish religion, such as the nature of God, the country of Israel and Jewish customs. It has developed ideas of inclusivity and has encouraged the involvement of women in liturgy. It has contributed to the notion that to be Jewish, one need only have one parent of the faith.

There are concerns about the future of Judaism, especially in the light of American figures that estimate that one in two Jews either does not marry or marries someone who is not Jewish. Antisemitism has made many fearful of their children, for example, appearing too overtly Jewish. Many young Jews are anxious to move away from Judaism that is defined by the persecution and suffering of the past. They seek a new type of Judaism that is relevant to them and appropriate for the age in which they live.

16

Christianity

'For God so loved the World that he gave his only Son,
that whoever believes in him should not perish but
have eternal life.'
John 3:16

Jesus Christ

That Jesus Christ actually existed is now acknowledged by
almost every historian as is his death by crucifixion under the
Roman prefect, Pontius Pilate (c. 36-39 AD). The religion
that was founded following his death holds that God took
on human form in the shape of Jesus, the Son of God, who
died on the cross but then rose from the dead and atoned for
the sins of those who believe in him. Christians take him to
be the Messiah who was foretold in the Hebrew scriptures
– the Old Testament to Christians. Indeed, the very name
of the religion – Christianity – comes from the Greek word
christós that is a translation of the Hebrew for 'messiah'. In
order to enter heaven, Christians must believe in Jesus and

be expectant of his return in what is known as the Second Coming. The time of this event is also aligned with the Day of Judgement. On the other hand, the life and teachings of Christ, as told in the New Testament, are generally disdained by historians, but, to believers, they are the absolute truth of what happened.

Christ was born, it is said, shortly before the death of Herod the Great (r. 37 BC-4 or 1 BC) who was king of Judea. At the time of his birth, the Jews were a subject people governed by local rulers appointed by the Emperor of Rome or directly by Rome. Many Jews opposed Roman rule, expressing this in outbreaks of rebellion. The Jews hoped for the day when God would come to their aid and would send a 'messiah' or saviour to liberate them. Some saw him as a spiritual figure, but others thought he would be a political leader and, indeed, movements grew around several such individuals, especially in Galilee.

Jesus' life story is told in the Gospels in which he is said to have been born in a stable in Bethlehem but brought up in Galilee. His birth takes place against the background of a census called by the Roman Emperor Augustus (r. 27 BC-14 AD) and, although his mother Mary is pregnant, she and her husband Joseph travel from Nazareth to his ancestral home in Bethlehem. Finding the town overcrowded due to the census, the couple are forced to seek shelter in a stable. Luke records that the new-born child, cradled in a manger, is visited by three shepherds but, although this is a humble place in which to come into the world, the birth has been heralded by angels, according to the Gospels. He would be the saviour and he has not been conceived naturally, but rather, by the power of the Lord.

There is a gap in the story of Jesus from infancy until he reaches the age of around 30. He would have had no academic grounding, being taught instead the skills of carpentry, but he would in all likelihood have also received an education at the local synagogue school. He is brought to notice after an encounter in Judea with John the Baptist who preaches penance and repentance for the remission of sins and foretells of the coming of someone more powerful than he. Jesus is baptised by John, John testifying that he 'saw the Spirit descend from heaven like a dove, and it remained on him'. After this, Jesus himself begins preaching and, when John is imprisoned, Jesus returns to Galilee to continue his work.

In the Gospels, we learn of Jesus' work – preaching, teaching and healing the sick. He and those who choose to follow him lead an itinerant life, depending on the generosity of others. Large crowds turn up for his sermons and many follow him everywhere he goes. He speaks with a simplicity that is absent from the sermons of other Jewish religious figures but people also flock to his events because he is said to be able to cure a variety of ailments and deformities, often with just a word or a laying-on of hands. He is also said to be able to drive out demons. He performs miracles such as calming a storm on a lake or making a small amount of food feed a large number of people.

He is accompanied everywhere by a devoted group of followers – his disciples. He teaches them and expects them to follow his teachings to the letter, to champion the ideals that he espouses and to rely on God for everything they require to live. After the ascension of Jesus to heaven, they, in turn, undertake preaching missions on their own. There are twelve disciples – also known as the Twelve Apostles – who were his closest followers and he taught them intensively so that when he was no longer around, they could continue his mission. They were Simon (Peter); Andrew; James (son of Zebedee); John; Philip; Bartholomew; Thomas; Matthew, James, son of Alphaeus; Simon the Zealot; Jude Thaddeus; and Judas Iscariot. Paul and Matthias also became apostles, Paul being called by the resurrected Jesus and Matthias elected by the others to replace Judas Iscariot.

Hugely popular with the ordinary citizens of Galilee, Jesus soon arouses the ire of the political leaders of the region who see him as a threat to the Jewish religious establishment. He behaves unconventionally, mixing with all races, professions and classes – even those on the edge of society. He values women, even those who were considered not respectable. Religious leaders also have issues with him because of his liberal attitude to matters such as the observance of the Sabbath, and his contention that purity of the heart is more important than ritual purification. He clashes continually in his statements with the traditions that had evolved over the centuries, expelling merchants and moneylenders from the Temple, even though the priests have encouraged them to do business there:

'And Jesus went into the temple of God, and cast out all them that sold and bought in the temple, and overthrew the tables of the moneychangers, and the seats of them that sold doves. And said unto them, It is written, My house shall be called the house of prayer; but ye have made it a den of thieves.'

It is worth remembering that all of this is said to be happening against the background of Rome's occupation of the region and Jewish leaders' fear that Jesus, with his huge following, is a destabilising influence. The people, meanwhile, increasingly view Jesus as their saviour, the man to free them from Roman hegemony. But, of course, he is not interested in politics and, as a result, his following decreases.

Jesus finally arrives in Jerusalem during the festival of Passover, riding on a donkey and welcomed by adoring crowds. He is eventually arrested by Jewish leaders after the Last Supper with disciples and after being betrayed by his disciple Judas, an act that he has prophesied. He is charged with blasphemy because of his claim to be the Messiah and the Son of God and is sentenced to death by crucifixion. The sentence needs to be backed up by a Roman conviction and, to this end, he is charged with sedition, the religious leaders persuading the Roman governor to confirm their sentence.

He is executed on the cross which would become a symbol for the faith he created and is interred in a tomb by a few followers. Two days later, when his disciples visit his tomb, they find it to be empty. A series of encounters with the risen Jesus follows in the next few weeks and, although he seems alive, he is able to appear and disappear suddenly, in various locations and even inside a closed room. In these meetings, he conveys to them once again what his life and his death symbolise, and reiterates the mission that he wants them to undertake to spread the word. Finally, he ascended to heaven: '…he was lifted up and a cloud took him out of their sight'.

Early Christianity

Christianity is a complex belief system and, with more than 2 billion adherents, is the world's largest religion. With its many diverse practices and offshoots, it can sometimes seem to be many different religions instead of one that is held together by a few core beliefs.

It began around the middle of the first century AD, as an offshoot of Judaism in the Levant region – known to Christians as the Holy Land – which at the time was under the suzerainty of the Roman Empire. The leaders of the early Church were the Apostles of Christ – his disciples – and for that reason, this era is known as the Apostolic Age, during which, as detailed in the New Testament, the former disciples of Jesus spread his teachings and small communities of Christians began to grow both in the countries of the Roman Empire and beyond its borders. Persecution by the authorities was rife at the time, and Christians were tortured and executed on a regular basis. Christians were subject to attacks and suspicion by Romans, and the Emperor Nero even made them scapegoats for the Great Fire that devastated Rome in 64 AD. This was the first instance of persecution by the Roman Empire of Christians, even though rumour had it that the fire was, in fact, started by Nero himself.

In Christianity's early years, it was still associated closely with Judaism, Christians often worshipping in synagogues, but gradually it became a separate religion. In these years, most of the major early Christian texts were being written. Despite the persecution by Rome, it began to spread because of the help it provided for people and probably also because its rites and beliefs were easy to understand, making it attractive to the poorer members of Roman society who flocked to it.

The period following the Apostolic Age is known as the Ante-Nicene Period. It dates from the end of the Apostolic Age, marked by the death of John the Apostle in Anatolia in around 100 AD, and lasted until the First Council of Nicaea that took place in 325. This was a critical time for Christianity, as it slowly began to grow and develop a unifying doctrine. The Christian canon was established and a number of heretical teachings were dispensed with. Most significantly, after the horrific persecution of Christians by the Roman Empire, the Roman Emperor Constantine I (r. 306 AD-337 AD) converted to Christianity and it received legal status in the Roman Empire. This was formalised by the Edict of Milan of 313 AD, drafted by Constantine and his rival in the Eastern Roman Empire, Licinius (r. 308 AD-324 AD) by which Christians were permitted to pursue their faith without oppression. Confiscated Church property was also returned. It would be another century before Christianity would become the official state religion of the Roman Empire.

In 325 AD, Emperor Constantine convened a meeting of Christian bishops in the Bithynian city of Nicaea (present-day Iznik in western Turkey). This significant conference was staged, amongst other things, in order to deal with a serious issue that was absolutely fundamental to the Church's teaching – the Arian heresy. Arius was a Christian ascetic from Alexandria who led a Christian congregation and taught that God and Jesus were not one and the same. He claimed that Jesus was subordinate to God the Father, stressing the supremacy of God and claiming that only He is eternal and almighty. Arius had created a huge controversy within the

Church that Emperor Constantine was anxious to end. He had already sent an emissary to Arius in an effort to resolve it. When that failed, he had no option but to convene the council. Representatives attended from all the dioceses of the Roman Empire, apart from Roman Britain. Constantine chaired the meeting and even took part in some of the debates which raged for two months before the majority of the 22 bishops present agreed on a creed which would become known as the Nicene Creed. It stated that God and Jesus were 'consubstantial' – 'one in essence'. Arius was excommunicated and, in an edict, Constantine took steps to ensure that his teachings be expunged:

'…if any writing composed by Arius should be found, it should be handed over to the flames, so that not only will the wickedness of his teaching be obliterated, but nothing will be left even to remind anyone of him. And I hereby make a public order, that if someone should be discovered to have hidden a writing composed by Arius, and not to have immediately brought it forward and destroyed it by fire, his penalty shall be death. As soon as he is discovered in this offense, he shall be submitted for capital punishment…'

The Nicene Creed established the Trinitarian version of Christianity which has become a cornerstone of the faith. God the Father, God the Son and God the Holy Spirit are consubstantial; the three are distinct but are one 'substance, essence or nature' and they are all divine.

The importance of the First Council of Nicaea to Christianity cannot be overestimated. It represented the first expression of an all-encompassing Christian orthodoxy and increased the unity of the young Church. As a result, its influence and membership grew substantially. In 381 at another important conference, the First Council of Constantinople, the Nicene Creed was revised and expanded.

Christianity in the Middle Ages

When the Roman Emperor Theodosius I (r. 379-392 in the East; and 392-395 in the entire Roman Empire) adopted Christianity as the official religion of his empire, five ecclesiastical centres were established at Rome, Constantinople, Antioch, Jerusalem and Alexandria. The Church became increasingly important in Western Europe, especially after the fall of the Roman Empire in 476 AD, representing stability for Europeans during a period of turmoil and often brutal violence. Meanwhile, Christian missionaries were busy, spreading the message of the Church across the continent, reaching as far as Anglo-Saxon Britain and Ireland. Dispatched by Pope Gregory the Great to bring the Church's message to the Anglo-Saxons, Augustine of Canterbury arrived in Britain in 596 and St Patrick is thought to have arrived in Ireland in 432 to carry out his missionary work. Monasteries were emerging as important religious centres around this time, becoming centres of learning as well as havens of spiritual life and they also began to wield political influence.

The seventh century changed everything, however. The rise of Islam in Arabia and its emergence as a social and political power, as well as a religious one, posed huge problems for Christianity and the next few centuries were difficult. Of particular concern were the divisions between the Church of Rome and the Eastern Patriarchy, centred on Constantinople. Somehow, despite their differences, the two branches of Christianity had managed to co-exist but the situation came to a head in 1054 and they split. For many years there had been differences and disputes between them – issues such as the source of the Holy Spirit, the use of leavened or unleavened bread in Holy Communion, the claim to universal jurisdiction of the pope in Rome and the place of the See of Constantinople in the organisation of the Church. There were political reasons, too, for the split. The last emperor of the Western Roman Empire was deposed in 476, leaving the Eastern Roman emperor with sovereignty over the entire empire. He held little sway in the West, however, where Germanic tribes were in control. This exacerbated the separation of the two entities, communication becoming difficult as fewer people spoke both Latin and Greek, the languages of the West and East, respectively. Differences in rites and doctrines began to appear and some kind of split seemed inevitable, even though it would take another few centuries for it to happen.

The rise of Islam did little to make the split any better for Christianity. The Seljuq Empire of Turkey had defeated the Fatimids who were based in Egypt in 1072 and they were less amenable to Christians and to pilgrims travelling in the Holy Land. They also harboured expansionist ambitions, a worrying set of circumstances for the rulers in the Eastern Roman Empire. Thus, when the Eastern emperor, Alexius I Komnenus (r. 1081-1118) asked the Roman Catholic Church for help in 1095, Pope Urban II (in office 1088-99) used that year's Council of Clermont to appeal for a Crusade against the Muslims. Addressing a large crowd of ecclesiastics and laymen, he said:

> '…this land which you inhabit, shut in on all sides by the seas and surrounded by the mountain peaks, is too narrow for your large population; nor does it abound in wealth; and it furnishes scarcely food enough for its cultivators. Hence it is that you murder one another, that you wage war, and that frequently you perish by mutual wounds. Let therefore hatred depart from among you, let your quarrels end, let wars cease, and let all dissensions and controversies slumber. Enter upon the road to the Holy Sepulchre; wrest that land from the wicked race, and subject it to yourselves… God has conferred upon you above all nations great glory in arms. Accordingly undertake this journey for the remission of your sins, with the assurance of the imperishable glory of the Kingdom of Heaven.'

The response was overwhelming and a series of invasions was launched that continued in waves until 1270. Such was the ardour aroused by Urban that several unofficial initiatives were launched in advance, the most notable being the People's Crusade, led by a charismatic French priest named Peter the Hermit (1050-1115). 40,000 mostly unarmed and untrained Crusaders, including women and children, were ambushed and massacred by the Turks at the Battle of Civetot in 1096. The First Crusade proper left for Jerusalem later in 1096. Led by a mixture of French knights and Norman nobles, it was far more organised and met with greater success. Several cities, including Antioch and Edessa, were taken before they captured the ultimate prize – Jerusalem. The inhabitants –

including Christians – were slaughtered. Instead of returning the land to the Eastern Roman Empire, however, the Crusaders instead founded four new states: the County of Edessa, the Principality of Antioch, the County of Tripoli and the Kingdom of Jerusalem. Godfrey of Bouillon, the Duke of Lower Lorraine (c. 1060-1100) was appointed the first ruler of Jerusalem but he never styled himself 'King'.

The Turks recaptured Edessa in 1144, leading Pope Eugene III (in office 1145-53) to call for the Second Crusade. This time, it struck on two fronts, one part of the force that was gathered attacking the Moors who had captured much of the Iberian Peninsula in 710. This struggle, known as the *Reconquista* would continue until 1492. Lisbon and other territories were won back. Meanwhile, in the east, the Crusaders proceeded to Jerusalem, for some reason ignoring occupied Edessa. They failed to take Damascus, defeated by the king of Mosul, Nur ad-Din (r. 1146-74) who went on to capture Syria. Jerusalem fell to the Muslims in 1187 following the defeat of the Crusader army by Sultan Saladin (r. 1174-93) at the Battle of Hattin.

Richard I 'the Lionheart' of England (r. 1189-99) and Philip II of France (r. 1180-1223) launched a Third Crusade in 1190. The Holy Roman Emperor, Frederick I Barbarossa (r. 1155-90), joined this force with his large army, but drowned before reaching the Holy Land. After some initial success with the capture of Acre, there were arguments over the division of the spoils and King Philip and Leopold V, Duke of Austria (1157-1194) took their armies home. Richard 'the Lionheart' defeated Saladin at the Battle of Arsuf but his depleted force was not enough to take Jerusalem.

After all this, European monarchs were reluctant to launch

another Crusade, but the pleas of Pope Innocent III (in office 1198-1216) were answered by an Italian count, Boniface of Montferrat (1150-1207) who led an army in the destruction of Constantinople after the emperor Alexius IV Angelus (r. 1203-04) failed to pay the Crusaders for overthrowing his uncle and installing him as ruler. Establishing a Latin Empire in Constantinople, they appointed Baldwin of Flanders (r. 1195-1203) as ruler. Large parts of the Byzantine Empire enjoyed Latin rule until 1261. As for the Holy Land, very few Crusaders actually made it that far. There were another four Crusades which all ended in failure – in 1216, 1228, 1248 and 1270.

The Reformation

Towards the end of the Middle Ages, the Catholic Church was an immensely important power in Europe, but there were issues that concerned many. Corruption and excess were rife in the Church and of particular concern was the granting of what were termed 'indulgences'. These were the means of reducing the degree of punishment that a sinner had to undergo and they were often granted in exchange for a donation of money. There were other manifestations of the corruption that pervaded the Church of Rome. Nepotism was rampant in the Vatican where friends and relatives of the pope – no matter who was in office – often gained positions for which they were manifestly unqualified. Things were little better out in the parishes where priests were failing to perform the duties required of them. Added to these was the fact that the Church seemed incapable of doing anything about the famines, plagues and wars that had ravaged Europe during the last two centuries.

A number of dissenters, such as Jan Hus (c. 1369-1415) and John Wycliffe (1320s-1384) had earlier railed against corrupt practices in the Church and Pope Julius II (in office 1503-13) eventually called the Fifth Lateran Council to deal with these practices. The Council ended in 1517 which turned out to be a year of some significance in European history. The central figure in the momentous events that were to follow was a professor at Wittenberg University named Martin Luther (1483-1546). Disgusted by the practice of indulgences, he authored a document named *Ninety-Five Theses* that he is said to have nailed to the door of All Saints' Church in Wittenberg on 31 October 1517, although this fact is disputed. It was a judicious moment as Germans were very much against the pope who had recently levied a tax on them. The struggling peasantry was disgusted by a dissolute clergy that owned vast tracts of land, lived a life of luxury and enjoyed great wealth.

Luther insisted that righteousness can only be attained through faith and the only source of faith is the Holy Scripture, that baptism and the Eucharist were the only worthwhile sacraments and worship of the saints and the Virgin Mary should be abolished. He said that priests did not need to be celibate and monastic orders and religious orders were pointless. Translated from Latin to German, printed and widely distributed, the *Ninety-Five Theses* caused a foment of religious discontent in Germany in its first two weeks of publication. Within two months it was doing the same throughout Europe.

Following unrest and initial violence, the princes of the German Empire gradually began to convert to Lutheranism, partly because their embrace of the new religion would weaken the hated Holy Roman Emperor Charles V (r. 1519-56), but also because they would be able to purloin Church property. They lost to the imperial army at the Battle of Mühlberg in 1547 but defeated the emperor a year later, securing the Peace of Augsburg which granted them an important right stating that whatever religious persuasion a prince was would be the same for his subjects.

Apart from Lutheranism, there were many other movements and doctrines across Europe. Amongst these was one led by the other major figure of the Reformation – the Frenchman John Calvin (1509-64). Forced to leave his country because of his ideas, Calvin relocated to Geneva where his thinking began to be put into practice. Worldly pleasures were banned, strict morality was imposed and there was harsh punishment for anyone breaking the rules. Calvinism quickly spread across Europe, taken up in England, Bohemia, France, Poland, Hungary and the Low Countries. In Scotland in 1561, another fiery preacher, John Knox, founded the Presbyterian Church, its teaching based on Calvinist principles. In England, the story of King Henry VIII's (r. 1509-47) trials and tribulations with the Catholic Church over his wish to divorce Catherine of Aragon and marry Anne Boleyn are well known. Pope Clement VII (in office 1523-34) refused permission for the divorce, but, despite this, Henry pronounced himself divorced in 1533. The result was his excommunication and eventually Henry's dissolution of the monasteries and establishment of the Church of England in 1536 with himself as head. His son, Edward VI (r. 1547-53) introduced Calvinism, but Catholicism returned under his successor, Queen Mary (r.

1553-58). Finally, Elizabeth I (1558-1603) who succeeded Mary, returned to Protestantism and, in 1563, Anglican doctrine was laid out in the *39 Articles*.

The Reformation seriously divided Europe and from its emergence many long-standing enmities grew. In France and the Holy Roman Empire, there were deep divisions between Roman Catholics and Protestants, divisions that led to a series of religious wars, both civil and between states. One of the most destructive of these conflicts was the Thirty Years' War that began in 1618 and was initially fought between various Protestant and Catholic states in the Holy Roman Empire. It gradually began to involve most of the great powers of Europe. Around eight million people lost their lives before its end in 1648.

The Counter-Reformation

The Catholic response to the Reformation lasted from around 1517 until the conclusion of the Thirty Years' War in 1648. Initially, there was little response from Rome to the surge of Protestantism in Europe, but during the Pontificate of Pope Paul III (1534-49) the papacy began to stir. Not that Paul was, himself, not guilty of providing positions for his family, but he realised the threat posed by Protestantism and convened one of the most important councils in the history of the Catholic Church – the Council of Trent. Meeting 25 times between 1545 and 1563 at Trent in northern Italy, this council launched the Counter-Reformation. The council condemned what it called the heresies of Protestantism and clarified Church doctrine.

Major reforms were introduced and the Catholic view of such things as scripture, original sin, the sacraments, the Eucharist and the veneration of saints was defined. It laid the foundations for modern Catholicism and constituted a strong riposte to Protestantism. The actions were left for the pope to make and he did so in the 1566 publication of a *Roman Catechism* that clarified doctrine but was also designed to improve the theological knowledge of priests. In 1568 a revised *Roman Breviary*, a book of prayers for daily use, was issued and two years later a revised *Roman Missal* appeared, detailing the text of the Mass to be said in Catholic churches. A further challenge to the rise of Protestantism was provided by the creation of new religious orders – Capuchins, Ursulines, Theatines and Carmelites, amongst others. The most important of the new orders was the Society of Jesuits, founded in 1534 by the Basque monk, Ignatius de Loyola (1491-1556). The Jesuits would become one of the most potent weapons the Roman Catholic Church employed against Protestantism and engendered fear amongst both Catholics and Protestants. For the Jesuits, the end justified the means.

Thus, by the end of the sixteenth century, Catholicism was enjoying something of a resurgence and Lutheranism began to decline in popularity, eventually becoming limited to Scandinavia and northern Germany, while Calvinism held sway in Scotland, Switzerland, Holland and western Germany.

Christianity in Modern Times

The political uncertainty of the eighteenth century had an impact on Christianity, especially in France where disgust for the Church contributed to the outbreak of the French Revolution in 1789. Christianity no longer held the power it did before the revolution. Across Europe, there were similar uprisings, causing huge problems for a Catholic Church that was being destabilised everywhere. Social and philosophical movements also challenged the position of the Church and religion in Western society. The German philosopher, Ludwig Feuerbach (1804-72) described God as the outward projection of an individual's nature:

'In the consciousness of the infinite, the conscious subject has for his object the infinity of his own nature.'

Another German philosopher, Karl Marx (1818-83), writer of *The Communist Manifesto*, opined that people had simply invented the idea of God as a way of making themselves feel better in the face of poverty and suffering. Deal with bad social conditions and there would be no need for religion. The founder of psychanalysis, Sigmund Freud (1856-1939), considered God to be no more than an illusion based on the infantile emotional need for a father-figure and that, although religion had been necessary in earlier times to keep humankind's violent nature in check, it could now be replaced by reason and science. Indeed, by the 1920s, having experienced the horrors of the First World War, many had discarded religion or believed that it was not intellectually acceptable.

By this time, too, the world's first openly atheist state – the USSR – had come into existence. This spread after the Second World War with Russian control of Eastern Europe where those nations under Russian influence followed suit. The collapse of communism, however, towards the end of the twentieth century, led to a more tolerant attitude towards religion in the nations of the Eastern Bloc. Islam also benefited from this new tolerance.

Types of Christianity

The term 'Protestant' is used to describe any Christian who does not accept the authority of the Catholic Church or the Eastern Orthodox Church. It is, of course, inadequate in that there are so many Christian denominations that deviate from these two churches.

The third largest branch of Christianity is the Anglican Church with some 85 million followers. Founded by Henry VIII, it includes the Church of England and affiliates such as the Episcopal Church of the United States. There are also many Anglican denominations in countries that were once part of the British Empire. It espouses several Protestant ideas but has also retained a number of Catholic elements, such as the way it is structured and even theological elements. As such, it sits between Catholicism and Protestantism. Its Supreme Governor is the monarch and the most senior cleric is the Archbishop of Canterbury.

In its Scandinavian and northern European enclaves, the Lutheran Church also retains elements of Catholicism but differs in one significant matter of doctrine. Lutherans believe that the only way to achieve salvation is through God's word, whereas Catholics believe that actions are also crucial. The Eucharist is also important to Lutherans who believe that it is the true body of Jesus Christ.

The Presbyterian Church differs from others in that each individual church is run by a group of elders who are elected to their positions. Councils that are also elected constitute the hierarchy of the Church. The doctrine of transubstantiation – the idea that the Communion meal is literally the body of Christ – is refuted by the Presbyterian Church as well as Reformed churches that base their theology on Calvinist philosophy. This is also one of the divergences between Presbyterianism and Lutheranism. There are around 40 to 50 million Presbyterians.

Yet another branch of reformed Christianity is Congregationalism which goes all the way back to the Puritans. Congregational churches are, therefore, most commonly located where Puritans settled, such as New England in the United States. The world's 5 million Congregationalists run their churches locally, the affairs of each church managed by the members of its congregation.

Methodism consists of a group of denominations, the history of which can be traced back to the teaching of the English cleric and theologian, John Wesley (1703-1791). Methodists emphasise the charitable and community elements of Christianity and have always been involved in missionary work to spread the message of God. There are between 60 and 80 million Methodists in the world.

As one would guess from the name, baptism is fundamental to the faith in the Baptist Church, which was founded from the teachings of the English cleric, John Smyth (c. 1570-

1612), although Baptists reject infant baptism. Indeed, it is adults only who are baptised, the ritual an affirmation of their faith and their commitment to God. The Baptist Church has been traditionally popular in the southern states of America, spread there by the populist religious movements that swept the United States in the eighteenth and early nineteenth centuries and have come to be known as the First and Second Great Awakenings respectively.

Some distinct Christian traditions have developed since the Reformation that cannot be strictly defined as Protestant. The Seventh-day Adventist Church grew out of the Millerite movement in the United States in the middle of the nineteenth century and was formally established in 1863. Seventh-day Adventists treat Saturday as their Sabbath and believe that the Second Coming of Christ is imminent. People should be preparing for this, they believe, because God is in the process of passing judgement on humanity. They claim that when we die we are not immediately judged as to whether we go to heaven or hell, but rather, our souls are unconscious, awaiting revival on Judgement Day. Its membership numbers around 20 million.

The Church of Jesus Christ of Latter-Day Saints – also known as the Mormon Church – was founded in the United States in April 1830 by Joseph Smith (1805-1844) who is believed by Mormons to have received their holy book, the *Book of Mormon*, from God. The *Book of Mormon*, they claim, contains the writings of ancient prophets, not in the Bible, who lived on the American continent between 2200 BC and 421 AD. Mormonism is itself broken down into several branches whose ideas on such matters as plural marriage, baptism for the dead and attitudes towards the Trinity differ. Mormons consider themselves to be Christians but there are a number of elements of their theology that have caused controversy over the years.

Founded in the late 1870s, Jehovah's Witnesses have a unique set of beliefs and methods of worship. The faith's eight and a half million followers believe that the destruction of the world in Armageddon is imminent and that humanity's problems can be solved only by the establishment of God's kingdom on earth. They reject Christian notions such as the Trinity and the inherent immortality of the soul and they believe that society is mired in sin. They ignore Christmas and Easter, believing them to be pagan festivals and engage in a great deal of missionary work.

Christian Beliefs

As with a number of religions, when we look at what Christians actually believe, there are a number of beliefs that are generally accepted, but there is debate about others. Most Christians accept the notion of the Trinity, that God is the Father, the Son and the Holy Spirit – 'one God in three Divine Persons'. They believe that Jesus Christ is divine, a human, but the Son of God and that he died on the cross before rising from the dead, sacrificing himself to atone for the sins of his believers. To them he is the Messiah – the saviour or liberator – talked of in the Old Testament. It is believed by most Christians that in order to be allowed to enter heaven after death, an individual must believe in Christ and believe that he will have a Second Coming, as detailed in the Nicene Creed:

'...he ascended into heaven and is seated at the right hand of the Father. He will come again in his glory to judge the living and the dead, and his kingdom will have no end... We look for the resurrection of the dead, and the life of the world to come.'

Amongst the things Christians believe about Jesus are the following: he was born of a virgin and had only one earthly parent – Mary; he was a human being who was also God; he never sinned or did any wrong during his time on earth; he was crucified, buried in a tomb and on the third day after his death, came back to life; he came back to life and, in fact, lives, and his spiritual body can be touched; he eventually ascended back to God; and he will return to earth again in the Second Coming.

Like adherents of the other Abrahamic faiths, Judaism and Islam, Christians are monotheistic, believing in one supreme God whom they consider to be omnipresent, omnipotent and omniscient. There are no other gods and God was the creator of the universe.

The teachings of Jesus are of paramount importance to Christianity. These teachings can, of course, be interpreted in different ways and this can be divisive amongst believers. However, his main messages to Christians were tolerance, love for others, obedience to God and redemption. For Christians, it is vital that they return to the Gospels to find guidance on how to live their lives according to Jesus. His message can be found in parables, discourses, such as the Farewell Discourse after the Last Supper, and in the miracles that he performed – cleansing lepers, for instance, or raising the dead. For Christians, these miracles are actual historical events supporting the fact that he was divine. Amongst the most powerful of Jesus's words are the Beatitudes that begin the story of the Sermon on the Mount, as written in the Gospel of St Matthew:

'Blessed are the poor in spirit: for theirs is the kingdom of Heaven. Blessed are those who mourn: for they will be comforted. Blessed are the meek: for they will inherit the earth. Blessed are those who hunger and thirst for righteousness: for they will be filled. Blessed are the merciful: for they will be shown mercy. Blessed are the pure in heart: for they will see God. Blessed are the peacemakers: for they will be called children of God. Blessed are those who are persecuted for righteousness sake: for theirs is the kingdom of Heaven. Blessed are you when others revile you and persecute you and utter all kinds of evil against you falsely on my account. Rejoice and be glad, for your reward in heaven is great, for so they persecuted the prophets who were before you.'

Christian Ritual and Practice

Most Christians take part in weekly services when the congregation gathers in its church to worship. In Christianity, the Sabbath is considered to be Sunday. The Roman Emperor Constantine the Great enacted the first civil law regarding this in 321 AD. His law did not actually mention Sunday by name, but referred to a day of rest – 'the venerable day of the sun':

'On the venerable day of the sun let the magistrate and people residing in cities rest, and let all workshops be closed. In the country however, persons engaged in agricultural work may freely and lawfully continue their pursuits; because it often happens that another day is not so suitable for grain growing or for vine planting; lest by neglecting the proper moment for such operations the bounty of heaven should be lost.'

For most Christians, one of the most important rituals is that of Communion, also known as the Eucharist (from the Greek *eucharistia* – 'thanksgiving'). This is symbolic of the Last Supper when Jesus shared a meal with his 12 disciples immediately prior to his arrest and crucifixion. During the meal, Jesus takes bread, breaks it and gives it to his disciples, saying: 'This is my body given to you.' In practice, Communion varies according to which branch of Christianity is involved, but it can generally be said to consist of the eating of specially made bread, representing the body of Christ, and drinking special wine, representing his blood.

Communion is symbolic of the sacrifice that Christians believe Jesus made for humanity and it also symbolises salvation. In some cases, such as in Catholicism, the rite is taken literally, with belief in the miracle of transubstantiation. The bread and wine, to Catholics, is literally the body and blood of Christ. For other branches of the faith, the rite is merely a metaphorical or symbolic act, although it is no less important.

Prayer is of great importance to Christians, either solitary prayer or prayers said in a group setting. It is viewed as a way of speaking directly to God, affirming belief, soliciting forgiveness for sins or for finding the answers to questions about how to lead an exemplary life. It can be said in a church in a highly formalised style, the congregation speaking together, or it can be said in a solitary situation, a personal communication with God.

Induction into Christianity is carried out by baptism. Just as Jesus was baptised by John the Baptist, so an individual is welcomed into the faith by being anointed with water. When a child is baptised, it is often called christening. The baptismal candidate can be immersed either partly or fully in water, depending upon the branch of faith to which he or she belongs, or water can be applied to the forehead, in a method called affusion.

Christianity Around the World Today

The growth of Christianity in non-Western cultures in recent times, has somewhat shifted its centre of gravity. Pentecostal Christianity has become phenomenally popular in South America, with around 40 million followers, and has led many to doubt the views of theological scholars who had been of the opinion that there would inevitably be a global decline in religious worship because of the growth of secular modernity. Indeed, the opposite appears to be happening and renders the decline of Christianity in the West something of a statistical anomaly.

The uptake of Christianity in Africa has gone even further to dispel the notion of a global decline. Christianity arrived in sub-Saharan Africa, expounded by missionaries during the nineteenth century. Africa is now on the verge of supplanting

Europe and North America as the nucleus of Christianity in the world. In fact, there are now far more Christians in Africa than in those two continents. Of the 80 million Anglicans in the world, for example, 20 million can be found in Nigeria and the numbers continue to grow inexorably.

Christians are very much in the minority in the countries of Asia, with some exceptions, such as South Korea, Singapore and the Philippines. There is growth in India, however, even against the background of Hindu culture. In China, Christianity was thought, some decades ago, to have no chance but religion in China has undergone a revival. Christianity was once regarded as too foreign to be taken up by the Chinese, but there are now estimated to be more than 30 million Christians in that vast nation, with a significant increase in the number of churches opened since 1949.

Women in Christianity

The roles of women in Christianity vary according to denomination. Traditionally, of course, men have occupied the leadership roles and, in the Roman Catholic and Orthodox Churches, only men can become priests or deacons and only men can become pope, patriarch or bishop. In Protestantism, most of the main denominations have begun to relax restrictions on women, and they may be ordained as ministers. In Pentecostal and Charismatic churches, generally speaking, women have always been ordained.

The Evangelical Lutheran Church in Germany introduced the ordination of women in 1976 and a large number of women came forward. Interestingly, this led to a decrease in the number of male ordinands. The Church of England, through its General Synod, decided to permit the ordination of women in 1992 and this has led to many women being ordained not only in England but around the world.

There are numerous women saints and Mary, the mother of Jesus Christ, is highly revered in all branches of Christianity. In Roman Catholicism, this is particularly the case, and Mary is described as the 'Mother of God'. Although she has always been venerated, the cult of the Virgin really took off in the twelfth and thirteenth centuries. As the Reformation began to make inroads in Europe, there was an antipathy towards Marian devotions in Europe, but veneration of her began to grow in Latin America, following Juan Diego's (1474-1548) reported vision of Our Lady of Guadalupe in Mexico City. Worship of the Virgin continued to grow through the seventeenth and eighteenth centuries and Marian culture still flourishes today.

17

Islam

'The only true faith in God's sight is Islam.'
Qur'an 3:19

The Prophet Muhammad

The Prophet Muhammad (c. 570 AD-632 AD) was born in Arabia in the second half of the seventh century and would create a religion that today has around 1.5 billion followers around the world. Followers regard Islam not as a new religion, but rather an eternal religion that is part of, and, indeed, the culmination of a series of communications from God to humanity. Muslims believe that there have been many prophets who have come to preach the truth about God to their people and Muhammad was the last one, come to spread the word of God to the Arab people and onward to the entire world. Like Christians and Jews, despite Islam's differences with them, Muslims believe that the God of Abraham is the one true God and that Muhammad's message was that we should submit to Him.

Muhammad was born at Mecca at a time when there were great changes in Arabia. Trade with other parts of the world was impacting society and the previous nomadic existence of Arabs was giving way to a more settled life. Mecca had become an important and powerful population centre, and the new Arab economy was controlled by wealthy merchants. These individuals would feel threatened by Islam when it first appeared. Religion was changing too, ordinary Arabs abandoning their old religious ways and their local shrines and beginning to worship, in larger groups, some of the more than 300 deities that existed.

Muhammad was born in about 570 into one of the leading merchant families of Mecca, but his branch of the family was by no means wealthy. Orphaned while still young, his early life was difficult but he appears to have been an intelligent, trustworthy and serious young man who was well liked by those he met. He was particularly interested in the injustices he saw in the society in which he lived, the oppression of the poor and the weak, the tribal wars, discrimination against women, slavery and economic exploitation. To consider these matters, he is said to have often gone into seclusion in a cave called Hira in Mecca. In 610, when he had once more retired to the cave, he received a vision in which the Archangel Jebreel (Gabriel) appeared, telling him that he was 'the Prophet of Allah'. Three years later, Muhammad began to spread the message of Islam publicly.

He gathered a few followers, but initially he was ridiculed. As the number of people following him grew, he began to draw the ire of Mecca's mercantile class, especially as he publicly condemned their materialism and greed. The small group of Muslims was persecuted and the merchants tried to kill Muhammad who now had many enemies, including some from amongst his own family. As a result, in 622, he led a *Hijrah*, an exodus from Mecca, taking his family and followers to Yathrib, a small town 300 miles to the north of Mecca. It would become known as Medina – 'the City of the Prophet'. In a city that was in turmoil, Muhammad became leader both in spiritual matters as well as in those of a political nature. He led a force against the commercial trade routes that were vital to the economy of it in order to weaken Mecca and make it more amenable to Islam. In 630, he defeated the Meccan army and took over the city. He would now be able to achieve his ambition to make Mecca the spiritual home of Islam and, in 632, the final year of his life, he led the first Islamic pilgrimage to Mecca. At Mount Arafat, to the east of the city, he delivered The Farewell Sermon in which he enumerated some of the core tenets of Islam – humanitarianism, egalitarianism, social and economic justice, righteousness and solidarity. He ended by saying:

'O People, no prophet or apostle will come after me and no new faith will be born. Reason well, therefore, O People, and understand words which I convey to you. I leave behind two things, the Qur'an and my example, the Sunnah, and if you follow those you will never go astray.

All those who listen to me shall pass on my words to others and those to others again; and may the last ones understand my words better than those who listen to me directly. Be my witness, O Allah, that I have conveyed your message to your people.'

A few months later, Muhammad fell ill and on 8 June 632, he died, aged 62 or 63.

Islam After Muhammad

Muhammad left behind both a religion and a nation which had begun as a federation of tribes but soon became a more formally organised body. The leader of the state was known as the caliph (*khalifa* in Arabic). The early caliphs continued Muhammad's practice of sending his troops on raids into Iraq and Syria from where they would return with booty. There was something of a power vacuum in the region, however, as the two great empires, the Persian and the Byzantine, had been at each other's throats for decades and were exhausted by the constant fighting. Soon, the Muslims were defeating their forces and extending their forward bases. Twelve years after the death of the Prophet, they had seized Egypt, Syria and Iraq and were advancing into Libya in the west. The people of these captured territories were given the status of 'protected minorities' by the Muslims. Those who were 'people of the book' – Christians, Jews, and those who believed in one God and had a written scripture – were allowed to govern themselves but had to pay taxes to a Muslim governor.

For the ensuing 100 years the Muslims continued to expand their territory. They occupied North Africa as far as the Atlantic and even crossed into the Iberian Peninsula. Their march into France was stopped by defeat at the Battle of Tours in 732. They stretched their empire as far as Constantinople but were unable to take any territory in Asia Minor. Persia and Afghanistan were taken and they got as far as crossing the Indus River into modern-day Pakistan. The peoples of these occupied territories continued to be made 'protected minorities', but they were not immediately forced to convert to Islam.

In 750, the Umayyid Dynasty that had been ruling the empire was supplanted by the Abbasid Dynasty which ruled from Baghdad, although they never had control of Muslim Spain which was ruled by an independent Emir, Abd ar-Rahman (756-788). Spain would remain independent of the caliphate for three centuries. Some outlying provinces were also lost but the Abbasids remained in power until 1258. During this period, a great deal of consolidation occurred. Work was done on developing Islamic law, the *Shari'a*. It was taken to a large extent from the Qur'an and from the collections of *Hadith* which were stories of Muhammad's actions, sayings and behaviour. Higher education consisted of the study of this law but, in other branches of education, the Qur'an, grammar and theological doctrine were studied. Greek philosophy, medicine and natural science were taught and many books were translated from Greek to Arabic. Generally, in science and the arts, it was a time of great advances.

Military expansion slowed after 750, apart from into India where it would climax in the Mughal Empire that lasted from 1556 until 1707. There, Hindus were considered to be 'people of the book', and most of them did not convert. Of course, Islam was also communicated abroad peacefully, as traders went about their business in West Africa and on the coast of East Africa. It also spread east from India, to the Philippines, Indonesia and Malaysia. It arrived in eastern China from Central Asia.

The religion's grip on Spain ended in 1492, after a gradual erosion of its power there, and it was around this time that European sailors began to make the great voyages that opened up the world and began to have an impact on the Muslim world. The Turkish Ottomans took over the caliphate in 1517 and expanded their territory, seizing much of southeastern Europe and the southern coast of the Mediterranean.

By the eighteenth century, the power of the Ottomans, along with the Mughals in India and the Safavids in Iran, was confronted by the rise of the superpowers of the West – the empires of the British, the Dutch and the French. Initially, the economic power of these nations made little impact on Muslims who were trying to regenerate their religion and their society. Reform was in the air, spreading along the pilgrimage routes to Mecca. Following the end of the First World War, however, the three great Muslim empires lay in tatters and were occupied or influenced by the European colonial powers which had won the war. Muslims were happy to benefit from the advances in science and technology that the Western powers brought with them, but they were opposed to the introduction of notions such as democracy and totally opposed, of course, to missionary efforts that threatened the Islamic faith. They were also against the secularisation of society that was the modern way. The traditional approach to religion was challenged by modernist reformers such as the Indian philosopher Syed Ahmad Khan (1817-98) and the Egyptian religious scholar Muhammad Abduh (1849-1905). Both men had travelled in Europe, and influences gleaned there informed their thinking. They argued that Muslims should not simply rely on the interpretations of texts provided by medieval clerics. Every Muslim, they insisted, could find the meaning of the scriptures for him- or herself. Their modernist thinking was guided by the lines to be found in *surah* 13:12:

'God does not alter what is in a people until they alter what is in themselves.'

The Qur'an, they argued, should be interpreted appropriately for the circumstances of the modern era. It is a debate that has raged from that day right up until the present time.

The twentieth century brought radicals, however, who changed the perception of Muslims in the West and helped to create tensions around the world. They contributed to the establishment of 'fundamentalism'. Two of the principal thinkers in this area were the Indian Muslim philosopher, Abul A'la Maududi (1903-79) and the Egyptian Islamic theorist Sayyid Qutb (1906-66) who both maintained that Muslims should live their lives strictly according to God's law. Both were scathing critics of Western morality, thoughts echoed by Ayatollah Khomeini (1902-89) who headed the government after Iran's Islamic Revolution of 1979.

The prevailing view, especially after the tragic events of 11 September 2001 when planes piloted by members of the Islamic terrorist group, al-Qaeda, were deliberately flown into buildings in New York and Arlington, Virginia, killing almost 3,000 people, is that two civilisations are colliding. Continued attacks in the name of so-called Islamic State and conflict in the Middle East have continued to create a deadly fault-line between the West and the Muslim world. Of course, Muslims themselves are very concerned by radicalism which is embraced by only a few and even conservative Muslim leaders have expressed concern about it. Extremists are reacting often to corrupt regimes and repression that are supported by the nations of the West and at the same time are taking up arms against what they see as terrible injustices by Western governments against Muslim communities in places such as Afghanistan, Chechnya, Iraq and Bosnia. They express their indignation against socio-political issues in religious terms.

Against this are reformers who are attempting to improve the situation of women in Muslim communities. But, although men and women can pray equally and the Qur'an accepts women's contributions to society in *surah* 3:195:

'I will deny no man or woman among you the reward of their labours.'

Modernist thinkers seek a loosening of the patriarchal nature of the Muslim family; the raising of the marriage age; the restriction of the male right of divorce, and making it less difficult for women to ask for a divorce.

Of course, the interpretation of God's word is still fundamental to Muslims but perhaps the emergence of female scholars and more educated women will contribute to change while still maintaining the harmonious and stable family life that ensures the wellbeing of the community.

Sunni and Shi'a

There are two main groupings of Muslims – Sunni and Shi'a – the result of a split after the death of the Prophet. The question was who was going to succeed Muhammad as leader of Islam. The faction that became the Sunnis, now making up around 85 per cent of Muslims, asserted that no one could succeed Muhammad, unless he was no more than a guardian of the Prophet's legacy. Therefore, he would be a caliph, responsible for the administration of the affairs of the community, according to the Qur'an and the example of the Prophet. The person so entrusted should, according to the Sunnis, be selected by the community from the men of Muhammad's family – the Quraish. Immediately after Muhammad's death, the succession passed to what are described as 'the four rightly guided caliphs' – Abu Bakr (r. 632-34), Umar ibn al-Khattab (r. 634-44), Uthman ibn Affan (r. 644-56) and Ali ibn Abi-Talib (656-61). These four were so close to the Prophet during his lifetime that their authority was unquestioned.

The caliphate, after 'the four rightly guided', took the form of a dynastic succession and it controlled the *Shari'a*, Islamic law. After the end of the caliphate in 1924, after 1,290 years, the responsibility for the law was considered to have been passed into the control of the Muslim states' governments.

Shi'a Muslims consider the *imam* – the worship leader of a mosque and of the Muslim community – to be the main focus of Islamic authority. Although Muhammad was the last prophet, completing the cycle of prophethood, they believe that he began 'the cycle of initiation' in appointing an *imam* as the one to follow him. In this figure was vested authority over how the Qur'an is interpreted. The first *imam* was Ali ibn Abi-Talib (600-61) who was Muhammad's cousin, but became his adopted son and later married his daughter, Fatimah (c. 609-632). The Shi'a believe that Ali inherited the spiritual abilities of the Prophet, and that he was infallible in matter regarding the Qur'an and in his position as leader of the Muslim community. This inheritance passed down to his sons, Hasan (625-70) and Husayn (626-80) and their descendants forever.

Most Shias now live in Iran and believe the cycle will be completed with the return to earth of the twelfth *imam*, known as the Mahdi, who will be the ultimate saviour of humanity.

Muslim Beliefs

There are six main tenets of Muslim faith. Muslims believe in one God – Allah (Arabic for 'the one God') – and also believe that Muhammad was his messenger. The Arabic word for the oneness of God is *Tawhid* and it embodies the concept of monotheism in Islam. There is no implication that Muhammad is divine and it is wrong to believe that Muslims worship the Prophet. Allah is eternal, omniscient and omnipotent; he has always existed and always will and he knows everything that is to be known.

In common with Christians and Jews, Muslims believe in angels and they are often referred to in the pages of the Qur'an. For Muslims, angels are devoid of free will and have to do what God tells them to. Muslims must also believe in the books God has sent to them. These include the Qur'an but it tells us that God also sent the Psalms (*Zaboor*), the Torah (*Taurat*) and the Gospel (*Injeel*). These books, they believe, were delivered to us in divine form originally but Jewish and Christian scriptures have been changed by humans through the centuries.

Muslims acknowledge a shared faith with and believe in the authority of all the Prophets who came before Muhammad, he being the last. In the Qur'an Noah (Nuh), Abraham (Ibrahim), Moses (Musa) and Jesus (Isa) are mentioned. They also believe in a Day of Judgement on which Allah will assess humankind. All life will be wiped out, then restored and judged. The Qur'an mentions the judgement of humanity frequently.

Finally, Muslims believe in the doctrine of *Qadr*, which is the Arabic word for destiny or fate. Some Muslims believe that God wrote down in the Preserved Tablet (*al-Lauh al-Mahfuz*) all that has happened and all that will happen. Allah has measured out the span of every individual's life, the bad things and the good and their achievements. This, however, does not mean that human beings don't have free will, the ability to make their own choices.

The Five Pillars of Islam

The Five Pillars are the five basic acts a Muslim is duty-bound to undertake. They are the very foundation of a Muslim life, although they are not mentioned in the Qur'an. Rather they are summarised in the *Hadith of Gabriel* which was revealed during a visit to Muhammad.

Shahada (belief) is the declaration of faith that there is only one God and that Muhammad is his messenger. The term incorporates the notion of bearing witness in public.

Salat (formal prayer) consists of five daily prayers that also include rituals of standing, bowing and prostration in a prescribed manner. There are minor variations between the Sunni and Shi'a traditions. The Qur'an is always recited, sometimes out loud and sometimes silently, and the ritual is always preceded by ablution (*wudu*), without which it is not valid. There are also optional prayers.

Sawm Ramadan (fasting in the month of Ramadan) entails

the abstention from food, drink and sexual intercourse from dawn to dusk for the month in question. This fasting helps Muslims to seek nearness and ask for forgiveness from God. Muslims are also required to be charitable during this month, over and above their normal charitable giving.

Zakat (charitable giving) is charitable giving that is based on how much money a Muslim individual has. It is viewed as purifying one's accumulated wealth and is mandatory for all Muslims who are able to make donations. It can also be an act of voluntary charity (*sadaqah*).

Hajj (pilgrimage to Mecca) is also mandatory. A pilgrimage to Mecca should be made at least once by every Muslim. If the individual lives too far away from the holy city for it to be practical or affordable, he or she is excused, although they must promise through prayer to make the journey sometime in the future. The *Hajj* commemorates the difficulties the Prophet Abraham and his family experienced in their lives. The Ka'ba, at the centre of Islam's most important mosque, the Al-Masjid Al-Haram, is the focus of the pilgrimage. It is a cubic room, built, according to the Qu'ran, by Abraham and his son Ishmael as a place of worship.

Islam places other obligations on its followers: to dress modestly and for women, to cover the hair and the neck; to participate in two communal holidays – Eid al-Fitr and Eid al-Adha; and to ensure that children are taught the Qur'an.

Sufism

The mystical Muslim movement of Sufism emerged as a response to what was seen as the secularity of the Umayyad

Caliphate that was in control of the Muslim Empire by the end of the seventh century. At the centre of this movement were intense meditation and esoteric ritual. Its approach to Islam was guided by the exhortation of the Prophet:

'To worship Allah as though you are seeing Him, and while you see Him not, yet truly He sees you.'

It took the name *tasawwuf*, meaning 'to dress in wool, or wear rough garb', reflecting the ascetic nature of the clothing worn by some adherents. In Britain and other English-speaking countries, the name Sufism is used to describe the movement, its members known as Sufis. They are members of different *turuq* – orders or congregations that have a grand master as leader. He is known as a *mawla* and is part of a direct line of teachers that can be traced all the way back to Muhammad. They hold gatherings (*majalis*) in places called *zawijas*, *khanqahs* or *tekke* at which they pursue their desire for *ihsan* (perfection of worship).

Sufism is often wrongly described as a sect of Islam. It is, rather, another aspect of it. It has been described by the fourteenth-century Islamic historian Ibn Khaldun as:

'...dedication to worship, total dedication to Allah most High, disregard for the finery and ornament of the world, abstinence from the pleasure, wealth, and prestige sought by most men, and retiring from others to worship alone.'

Sufism is all about the purification of the inner self or the spirit in order to find God. Sufis believe that they are practising Islam in its original form which leads to a degree of scepticism towards them from orthodox Muslims, some of whom consider that they are too heavily influenced by various other faiths. Sufism has indeed adopted features of mystic disciplines found in other non-Muslim religions. However, it has been important in shaping and guiding Islamic thought throughout its history and it helped to take Islam to Africa, India and the Far East.

The Qur'an

The Qur'an is the most important Muslim holy book, representing the word of God, as passed to Muhammad. Written in the old Arabic dialect, it is believed by Muslims to have been revealed to Muhammad by the Archangel Gabriel over a period of 23 years. It was written down by several of the Prophet's companions and was compiled after his death by these companions. A standard version was created by the Caliph Uthman, the third of the 'rightly guided caliphs'.

The Qur'an consists of 114 chapters, each of which, except one, begins with the sentence *Bismillahir rahmanir Raheem* – 'in the name of Allah the most merciful and the most kind'. These are the words that should be in a Muslim's mind whenever he or she is about to do something. The *surah Baqarah* (The Cow) is the longest chapter in the book with 286 verses and the shortest is *surah Al-Kawther* (Abundance) with a mere three verses. The book's chapters are not presented in chronological order, according to when they were revealed to the Prophet. Instead, apart from the first chapter – The Opening – they are in order of length, the longest first.

Its contents make little separation between the secular and

the sacred, its themes incorporating the difference between right and wrong, and exhortations to obey God and also to fear him. It contains parables that clearly teach the reader a lesson and there are passages that describe the experience of Muhammad when he was having his revelations. Some passages deal with legal matters, giving guidance in the organisation of the Muslim community and others provide encouragement to Muslims who at the time were undergoing challenges. Biblical characters and events appear and there are elements of Muhammad's life that enable us to compile his own story.

In order to make the Qur'an more accessible to Muslims who want to read it during the course of one month, it is divided into 30 parts which are known as *juz*. This is done particularly during the month of Ramadan. It has, of course, been translated into many languages, but Muslims have to read it in Arabic, even if that is not their language. Reading the Qur'an brings rewards to a Muslim and memorising it is even more highly valued as an act of piety.

Independent Belief Systems

The Baha'i Faith

The Baha'i Faith was created by a merchant, Sayyid 'Ali Muhammad Shirazi (1819-50), who was born in Shiraz in Persia – present-day Iran. At the age of 24, he claimed to be a Messenger of God, adopting the name 'the Báb', meaning 'Gate' or 'Door'. He taught and composed letters and books, reiterating his claims to be a Prophet of a New Age and attracting thousands of followers. Fiercely opposed to him, Iran's Shia clergy and the government of the country began to persecute his supporters who were known as 'Bábis', and around 3,000 of them were killed. Eventually, aged just 30, the Báb was himself arrested and executed by firing squad.

Three years after his death, one of his followers, Mirza Husayn 'Ali Nuri (1817-92), who had taken the name Bahá'u'lláh, ('the Glory of God'), was sent into exile in Baghdad which was at the time a part of the Ottoman Empire. There, in 1863, he declared the Baha'i Faith, professing to be the bearer of a new message from God. He claimed that basing his teaching on previous religions, he would create world unity. Once again, however, the authorities in Baghdad saw him as a danger to the stability of the empire and he was exiled to Edirne and then Akko (Acre, in present-day Israel) where he remained until his death in 1892. He was buried there and his shrine is now the holiest site for followers of the religion he created.

Before his death, he appointed his eldest son, 'Abdu'l-Baha (1844-1921), as head of the Baha'i Faith. In 1911 and 1912-13, 'Abdu'l-Baha made trips to Europe and North America to visit communities of Baha'i followers that had been established there. Following his death in 1921, he was succeeded as leader of the faith by his grandson, Shoghi Effendi (1897-1957) who spent time reforming the organisation and administration of the Baha'í Faith in order to take it to parts of the world where it was not yet established. Baha'í followers acted as unpaid missionaries, moving to those places and trying to increase the faith's following. Shoghi Effendi took a particular interest in the development of the Baha'í World Centre on Mount Carmel in Haifa, Israel. No leader followed Shoghi Effendi after his death in 1957 until the Universal House of Justice was elected, as stipulated by Bahá'u'lláh in his writings. It became the supreme authority of the Baha'í Faith and remains so to this day.

Followers of the Baha'í Faith have endured persecution in some Muslim and Communist countries. Probably the worst was enacted in Iran after the Iranian Revolution of 1979 in which the monarchy was overthrown and an Islamic Republic was created. A large number of Baha'ís were executed and a great many also disappeared, presumably also executed. In spite of this, the faith has continued to grow around the world and its 5 million followers can be found in every country apart from Vatican City. The largest following is in India but large numbers of Baha'ís can also be found in Latin America, Southeast Asia and Africa. Between 1910 and 2010, it was estimated by one source to be the fastest-growing religion in the world.

Baha'í Beliefs and Practices

Baha'ís believe in three core tenets – the unity of God, the unity of religion and the unity of humanity. It is a Universalist faith that claims that all religions and prophets are merely different manifestations of the same God, different in order to respond to the needs and practices of different peoples in different situations and with different experiences of the world. In the spirit of our current age, the Baha'í Faith is inclusive – probably the most inclusive religion in existence – embracing both Abrahamic and *dharmic* prophets and messengers as manifestations of the one God. Baha'ís have even assimilated rituals and prayers from other religions. They believe that God reveals His will to mankind on a regular basis through messengers or prophets and each messenger starts a religion. This is the opposite of what most other faiths teach. They believe that their prophet or messenger is the last one. For the Baha'í, each messenger reveals more to humankind than the previous one and reveals to his followers according to their societal and environmental conditions.

Although Baha'ís see men and women as being equal, in some aspects of life, they see them as different. They believe they have different skills and capabilities and, of course, women are the bearers of children. Thus, Baha'ís emphasise education for women as a priority as they will be the first teachers of their children and all posts are open to women apart from those at the Baha'í Universal House of Justice. In fact, education is fundamental to the Baha'í Faith and teachings promote moral and spiritual education. Baha'í education also focuses on the arts, trades and other professions.

For Baha'ís, science and religion must be in harmony, thus refuting the customary dichotomy between the two. 'Abdu'l-Bahá explained that science without religion leads to materialism, and religion without science leads to superstition. He also asserted that the reasoning powers that are required to understand science are equally necessary to the understanding of religion.

Bahá'u'lláh taught that the great number of different languages in the world was a barrier to communication and that, until a language spoken by all is developed, the unity of the world that Baha'ís seek would be impossible. The faith also teaches the need to do away with the extremes of wealth and poverty that exist and that the rich have an obligation to take care of the poor. 'Abdu'l-Bahá stated that wealth was not inherently evil and could be used to help others.

Baha'í communities meet once every nineteen weeks for what is called the Nineteen-Day Feast. This is split into three sections – devotion, consultative and social. There are no set rituals and the time can be tailored locally. If there are enough Baha'ís locally, meetings will take place in a House of Worship; if not, they take place in the homes of followers.

Both Bahá'u'lláh and 'Abdu'l-Bahá composed prayers that are used by followers of the Baha'í Faith. Three prayers written by Bahá'u'lláh have achieved a ritual status in the faith and all adherents must recite one of these daily. There are also prayers written by these two leaders that have specific uses for funerals, weddings and other ceremonies.

Baha'í Sacred Writings and Authority

Bahá'u'lláh wrote several key works and many letters that are known to Baha'ís as 'Tablets'. These were replies to questions from both followers and non-followers. There are some 100 volumes of such letters. Of greatest importance to Baha'ís, however, are Bahá'u'lláh's *Kitab-i-Aqdas* (The Most

Holy Book) and the *Kitab-i-Iqan* (The Book of Certitude). The former, also known as the 'Charter of the future world civilisation', contains laws, religious practices, mysticism, ethics and prophecies while the latter deals with theological issues and talks about the prophecies of the Bible and the Qur'an. 'Abdu'l-Bahá wrote on many subjects and his writings as well as those of his father, Bahá'u'lláh are acknowledged as scripture by Baha'ís.

In areas that are not dealt with by scripture, the Baha'í House of Justice steps in. Although its decisions are authoritative, its rulings can be changed or even repealed by a later House of Justice. Rather than depend on legislation, however, the House of Justice encourages Baha'ís to make their own decisions, using their own spiritual and moral standards.

Atheism

It may seem strange to include atheism in a book about religion, but as a belief in itself, and its direct opposition to belief in God, it is important that it is explained. Basically, it means a lack of belief in deities and even an outright rejection of belief that God or other divine forces exist. The term, in fact, originated before the fifth century BC and comes from the Greek *atheos*, meaning 'without gods'. Originally, in ancient times, it was used to describe those who had rejected the gods or people who had been forsaken by the gods. The term 'atheism' was first used in the sixteenth century and it was during the Age of Enlightenment in the eighteenth century that certain people began to describe themselves as atheists. The French Revolution, of course, was a hotbed of atheism, the first political movement in history to speak of the supremacy of reason over religious belief. As a concept, atheism is accepted by religions such as Buddhism, Hinduism and Jainism.

Arguments in favour of atheism vary greatly, but they include the assertion that human beings can easily create their own standards for living a good and proper life without divine help. Some atheists argue that science has proved that there was no divine creator of the universe. A common argument is that there cannot possibly be a God in a world where so many evil things happen. There is an argument that, if there is a divine presence, then he must have been created. That leads to an infinite number of divine creators which defies logic.

Atheism does not preclude living an ethical and good life, and atheists would claim that the creation of their own moral standards gives them control over their lives.

Agnosticism

Agnostics hold the view that the existence of God is unknown and unknowable or, in the words of the American philosopher, William L Rowe (1931-2015):

'...agnosticism is the view that human reason is incapable of providing sufficient rational grounds to justify either the belief that God exists or the belief that God does not exist. In so far as one holds that our beliefs are rational only if they are supported by human reason, the person who accepts the philosophical position of agnosticism will hold that neither the belief that God exists nor the belief that God does not exist is rational.'

So, rather than saying that agnostics are those who neither believe nor disbelieve in God, it is probably more accurate to describe them as individuals who think that the human mind is not capable of confirming or denying the existence of God.

It is possible to be agnostic, but at the same time be a theist or even an atheist. English naturalist, Charles Darwin (1809-82), for instance, who had actually studied to be an Anglican clergyman, eventually developed doubts in his faith, but carried on being involved in church affairs, even though he stopped attending church. He said that it would be 'absurd to doubt that a man might be an ardent theist and an evolutionist'. In 1879, he wrote: 'I have never been an atheist in the sense of denying the existence of a God. I think that generally... an agnostic would be the most correct description of my state of mind.'

As with atheism, agnosticism does not have a central doctrine or core tenets. And as in atheism, agnostics create their own codes of conduct.

Faith Systems Based on Nature

Around the globe there are many people who base their religious feelings on nature. People who believe thus, often describe this type of belief as pagan or neo-pagan, but pagan is in itself a fairly pejorative term and many prefer not to associate themselves with it. This type of religious practice harks back to the time before Christianity became predominant in Europe and amongst the faiths that indulge in this type of practice can be listed Druidism, Wicca, Goddess Spirituality, Heathenism and many others. Such faiths may show reverence for the natural world and they can be animist – the belief that objects, places and creatures all possess a spiritual essence. They can also be poly- or pantheistic and can often be heavily influenced by the folklore of the local area. These faiths are often focused on individualism and mainly believe that you may do whatever you want as long as it does no harm.

Rastafarianism

Rastafari or Rastafarianism is an Abrahamic religion and also a social movement which emerged during the 1930s in Jamaica. As a religion, it has no central authority. Rastafarians, as its members are called, interpret the Bible in a specific way, the result known as 'Rastalogy'. They believe in one God, called Jah by them and believe that he resides partly within each person. Of crucial importance to Rastafarians is the former Emperor of Ethiopia, Haile Selassie I (r. 1930-74) who is seen by Rastafarians as either the Second Coming of Jesus or God incarnate. Interestingly, the emperor chose to keep his distance from the movement.

Rastafari developed amongst the poor of Jamaica in the 1930s as an antidote to British colonial culture, emerging from the Back-to-Africa movement that was promoted by black nationalist leaders such as Marcus Garvey (1887-1940), the head of a mass movement called Pan-Africanism. It came from the assertion by several clergymen in Jamaica that the coronation of Haile Selassie in 1930 was the fulfilment of a Biblical prophecy. There was violence between the authorities and Rastafarians in the 1950s but the 1960s and 1970s brought a greater profile for the movement due to its championing by reggae musicians such as Bob Marley (1945-81). With Marley and Selassie gone by the 1980s, Rastafari waned in popularity.

Rastafarianism claims Africans as the chosen people of God who have been suppressed by European colonialists and attitudes. One day, they believe, they will return to their rightful position with the help of Jah. They eschew material things in order to attain a high spiritual consciousness and aim also to achieve this by not cutting their hair and by using marijuana as a sacrament. It is smoked during what are called 'groundings' – the establishment of relationships between like-minded practitioners, presided over by an elder – but many smoke it all the time. They are vegetarians, do not drink alcohol and refer to the material culture of the world as 'Babylon'. Zion, on the other hand, signifies Ethiopia to which Rastafarians long to be repatriated.

There are between 700,000 and a million Rastafarians in many different regions and in many of the major population centres of the world.

Santeria

Santeria – Spanish for 'worship of saints' – is an Afro-American religion of Caribbean origin that developed during the Spanish Empire amongst West Africans who had been taken to the Caribbean to work as slaves. Practised mainly in Cuba, Puerto Rico, the Dominican Republic, Mexico,

Panama, Colombia and United States, it is influenced by Roman Catholicism. Emerging in Cuba initially, it spread beyond the Caribbean to the United States and elsewhere after the Cuban Revolution. It uses the sacred language Lucumí, a type of Yoruba, and is based on the idea that there is a single god whose name is Olodumare. Important figures are three Orishas, powerful spirits who can be linked to Catholic saints. Adherents are expected to make sacrifices to these beings in order to achieve the destiny that God planned for them.

Santeria has neither a central creed nor a central organisation. Neither does it have a written tradition. Instead, there is a complex initiation process that passes on details of rituals and beliefs from one adherent to another. Priests are called Santeros and Santeras and it is they who have the power to control the Orisha.

Through Santeria rituals, people can remain in contact with Orishas and, during such ceremonies, there is drumming and dancing, and followers speak and eat with the Orishas. The rituals take place in rented halls as there are relatively few buildings actually devoted to the faith. Or they may take place in the homes of followers where altars will have been installed. During certain rituals, Orishas are said to meet believers.

Animal sacrifice plays a large part in Santeria. It is used during initiation ceremonies and in the ordination of priests. The blood of the animals is offered to the Orisha in order to foster a relationship with the spirit. Such sacrifices will be made at major events in believers' lives, such as births, marriages and deaths.

Candomblé

An African-Brazilian religion, Candomblé, which translates as 'dance in honour of the gods', developed amongst Africans who were transported to Brazil to work as slaves. It derives from the beliefs of the Yoruba, Fon and Bantu peoples but has also assimilated some Roman Catholic elements. Music and, as its translated name would suggest, dance are important to Candomblé ritual.

When slaves arrived in Brazil, slave owners tried to convert them to Christianity, firstly because their religion obliged them to, but also because they hoped it would render the slaves more submissive. Many were forced to accept the faith, and pretended to embrace it, but at the same time, they remained faithful to their own gods. In Brazil, as in the Caribbean, adherents of Candomblé saw a link between the Catholic worship of saints and their own faith. Candomblé followers used Catholic meetings to practise Candomblé and to plot rebellion against their masters. There was also a synergy between transported Bantu people and Brazil's indigenous people and this link reintroduced them to ancestor worship, as had been practised back in their homelands.

Of course, the Catholic Church was appalled by Candomblé and adherents were ruthlessly persecuted. This persecution persisted until the 1970s when a law that meant police permission was required for public ceremonies was revoked. Since then Candomblé has become even more popular and there are as many as 2 million practitioners in Brazil. To many, it has become a way to recapture the cultural heritage that was stolen from their ancestors centuries ago.

Candomblé is similar to Santeria in that believers worship one god called Olodumare who is served by lesser gods – Orixas, Voduns and Inkices. Orixas are ancestors who have become gods and Voduns and Inkices are spirit gods. Everyone has his or her own personal Orixa to protect them and guide them. During ceremonies, intricately choreographed dances are performed in order to become possessed by each ancestor spirit.

Individuals must fulfil their own destinies to the utmost of their abilities but any evil committed will come back eventually to hurt the perpetrator. The moral code of believers is regulated by Baba Egum, as ancestor spirits are known.

New Religious Movements

It is difficult to be precise as to what the word 'new' means in the context of religion. Some suggest that it should be applied to religious movements that have emerged since the end of the Second World War while others spread the net a little more widely, ascribing the description to those that have developed in the last century and a half.

They can, of course, be controversial, and in the media are often referred to as 'cults', especially when there are sensational events surrounding them. There is a long list of events in which a group's activities have ended in tragedy – David Koresh and the Branch Davidians at Waco, Texas: Jim Jones and the Peoples Temple at Jonestown in Guyana; the Solar Temple in Canada and Switzerland; Heaven's Gate in California, to name but a few. The perception created by such events is a terrifying one, but, of course, given the sheer number of new religious movements, the percentage that go wrong is very low.

Because there are so many new religious movements – an estimated 10,000 in Africa; 3,000 in the United States and more than 500 in the United Kingdom – only a few of the better-known, or more notorious ones can be described here.

A number of new Christian movements emerged in the nineteenth century, some of which still exist today or which spawned churches still practising. The activities of the American Baptist preacher William Miller (1782-1849), for instance, led to Adventism and the establishment of the Seventh-day Adventist Church. Miller prophesied that the Second Coming would happen on 22 October 1844. A national movement developed that even spread to Great

Britain. The failure of his prediction has become known as the Great Disappointment.

The creation of Mary Baker Eddy (1821-1910), Christian Science developed from her 1875 bestselling book, *Science and Health with Key to the Scriptures*. She claimed that poor health is an illusion that can be cured only by prayer and, with 26 followers, she established the Church of Christ, Scientist in 1879. In 1894, the movement's main church, The First Church of Christ, Scientist, was constructed in Boston. At one time the fastest growing religion in the United States, it had 270,000 adherents by 1936, although it had declined to 100,000 by 1990. Eddy described her church as a return to 'primitive Christianity and its lost element of healing'. Followers believe that the material world is an illusion. Although not eschewing medical care completely, Christian Scientists believe that prayer is at its most effective when it is not combined with medicine. This can leave practitioners open to prosecution for manslaughter or neglect and several have been prosecuted and convicted when children or loved ones have died for want of medical treatment.

The hippie movement of the 1960s, with its communal living, disdain for material possessions and drug-taking, led to a wave of new churches. The Love Family, for example, began in 1968 as the Church of Jesus Christ at Armageddon, having been founded by Paul Erdman who changed his name to Love Israel. Initially just a small communal household, it expanded and within ten years had a number of properties and businesses. Property in Washington State, Alaska and Hawaii was given to the church although it was either sold or won back in litigation. 'Love Israel' was a play on the phrase 'Love is real', a key phrase from the 1960s and every member of the group took the surname Israel. The group remains together on the shore of the Columbia River in Washington State, although their leader died in 2016.

One of the more controversial new religious movements was also spawned during the 1960s. David Berg (1919-94), who also styled himself 'Moses David', 'The Last Endtime Prophet' and 'King', founded Teens for Christ in 1968, changing its name to the Children of God a year later. Initially, it recruited new members using a type of evangelism they described as 'Flirty Fishing', in which female followers were encouraged to 'show God's love' by having sex with potential recruits. This later led to accusations of sexual relationships with minors. Berg communicated with followers through letters, known as 'Mo Letters' which contained messages and spiritual guidance and the group expanded. By 1972, there were 130 COG communities around the world. The name was changed to The Family in 1982 and in 1995, after Berg's death, Karen Zerby, also known as Mama Maria and Queen Maria, took over the leadership. In 2004, the name was changed once more, to The Family International. TFI believe that they are fighting a spiritual war against the forces of evil and are helped in this by a variety of angels including the goddess Aphrodite, Merlin and celebrities such as Elvis Presley and Audrey Hepburn.

The Unification Church is a spiritually-based movement founded by the Korean entrepreneur Sun Myung Moon (1920-2012). Moon insisted that he was marking 'the end of religion' and that his organisation was not a church. In fact, he said, the name Unification Church was given to it by others and not by him nor its members. Followers believe that Jesus Christ appeared to their late leader in 1935 when he was 16 and asked him to finish his work. He preached in northern Korea and founded the Unification Church in 1954 as The Holy Spirit Association for the Unification of World Christianity. Through time, the church grew in membership across the world and Moon moved to the United States in 1971. He and his wife Hak Ja Han Moon (born 1943) – who became leader after her husband's death – are perceived by the church's membership as the new messiahs. In 1994, Moon changed the organisation's name to the Family Federation for World Peace and Unification and announced that it would be working with members of other religious organisations on common objectives such as matters of sexual morality and the reconciliation of people of all races, ethnicities and religions. The organisation is famously anti-communist and even supported President Richard Nixon during his troubles in the early 1970s. It has been accused of brainwashing members who are welcomed into the church through the Blessing ceremony, a mass wedding in which members are married to each other.

Hinduism

There are a number of successful new movements that derive from India. Hindu holy men have been visiting the West since Vivekananda (1863-1902), the pupil of Indian mystic and guru, Ramakrishna (1836-86) in the nineteenth century, introducing people to the Indian philosophies of Vedanta and yoga. Paramahansa Yogananda (1893-1952) moved to America in 1920, using his organisations, the Yogoda Satsanga Society of India and the Self-Realization Fellowship, to introduce millions of westerners to meditation and Kriya Yoga. Many have followed, sweeping up Western converts. Meher Baba (1894-1969) claimed to be God in human form and maintained silence from 1925 until his death in 1969; Sri Chinmoy (1931-2007) advocated prayer and meditation as the way to find a path to God; and AC Bhaktivedanta Prabhupada (1896-1977) launched the International Society for Krishna Consciousness (ISKCON) in 1966, popularly known as the 'Hare Krishna movement'.

Maharishi Mahesh Yogi (1918-2008) insisted the organisation he founded to spread the technique of Transcendental Meditation was not a religion. He started teaching it in 1955 and achieved fame and popularity for his technique when he became guru to celebrities such as The Beatles, The Beach Boys and others. He is said to have trained 40,000 TM teachers and taught his discipline to 5 million people. He opened schools and universities around the world and his organisation became immensely wealthy. In his technique, students are allotted a mantra that they have to use twice daily.

Sathya Sai Baba (1926-2011) established the Sathya Sai Organisation that has 1,200 centres in 126 countries. He was famous for his miracles, including making things materialise and healing. In 1963, he suffered a stroke and four heart attacks and was paralysed down one side. He is said to have healed himself in front of an audience of thousands in his ashram, Prashanti Nilayam. Followers believe him to have been God incarnate and make pilgrimages to his ashrams in India.

Bhagwan Shree Rajneesh (1931-90) created a religious movement known as the Rajneesh movement whose members dressed in orange clothing, leading to them being called 'the orange people'. He was opposed to socialism and Hindu religious orthodoxy and had a liberal attitude to sexuality, earning himself the nickname in the media of the 'sex guru'. In 1981, he set up his own 'enlightened city' in Oregon, named Rajneeshpuram. In 1984, a leading group of his followers poisoned the salad bars of ten local restaurants in The Dalles, Oregon in order to stop people from voting in local elections, thus allowing their candidates to win. 751 people fell ill in what was one of only two bioterror attacks in the USA since the Second World War. Although Rajneesh was not prosecuted for this crime, he was arrested in Charlotte, North Carolina and charged with violations of immigration laws. He was given a ten-year suspended sentence and banned from the United States for five years. Other countries denied him entry and he returned to Puna in India where he died in 1990.

New Buddhist Movements

Zen Buddhism took off in the West in the 1950s and 1960s, helped by the writings of DT Suzuki (1870-1966). The counter-culture of America and Europe embraced Zen. Hippies and beatniks responded to its philosophy and created their own anarchic version. New movements have also emerged from the various traditions of Buddhism.

Buddhist Modernism provides new interpretations of Buddhist thought and practice. The internalisation of Buddhist gods makes such a version of Buddhism attractive to Western practitioners. Furthermore, much of the trappings of

Buddhism, such as idol worship, are de-emphasised to make it accessible to Western minds. There are a number of Buddhist Modernist movements – Humanistic Buddhism, Engaged Buddhism, Navayana, Secular Buddhism and Dharma Drum Mountain, to name just a few. Tibetan Buddhist missionaries are hard at work in the West drumming up new recruits to the religion.

The Vipassana movement champions modern Theravada Buddhism. Vipassana is an ancient Buddhist discipline that enjoyed a revival in Myanmar and Thailand in the twentieth century. It attempts through meditation to give the practitioner insight into the three marks of existence – impermanence (*anicca*), suffering (*dukkha*) and non-self (*anatta*) – thus helping to attain wisdom and awakening. It is practised by many lay people in the West.

The New Kadampa Tradition is a global movement founded in England in 1991 by Buddhist monk Kelsang Gyatso (born 1931). It currently has more than 200 centres in 40 countries. Gyatso has made Buddhist meditation more accessible to people in the modern world. Gyatso's championing of the entity, Dorje Shugden, is controversial within traditional Buddhist circles, especially as the Dalai Lama has forbidden its use.

Soka Gakkai International (SGI) was founded in 1975, its teachings deriving from Nichiren Buddhism, devised by the teacher Nichiren (1222-82), using the Lotus Sutra. SGI is the largest of the new Japanese religions, and the centre of its devotional practice is the chanting of the mantra *Nam Myoho Renge Kyo*, believed to possess great power, and to give material and spiritual benefits to the practitioner. The group has proved controversial in Japan where it is viewed with suspicion and it has a close association with Komeito, a centre-right political party.

Engaged Buddhists apply what they derive from meditation to social, environmental and political issues. Based on the teachings of the Vietnamese Zen Buddhist teacher, Thich Nhat Hanh (born 1926), Engaged Buddhism has gained great popularity in the West through organisations such as the Buddhist Peace Fellowship and Buddhist Global Relief.

China

In the second half of the twentieth century, there was a resurgence of interest in the meditative exercises known as *Qigong*. This was a set of exercises that involved slow movement, meditation and regulated breathing. Such exercises have long been practised by Daoist martial artists, Buddhist monks and scholars of Confucius. The objective is to improve spiritual, moral and physical wellbeing. In the 1950s, the Communist government viewed *Qigong* as a way to improve the nation's health and fitness. Following the death of Mao Zedong, millions of Chinese citizens took up *Qigong*. It began to fill the spiritual vacuum left by Mao's death and men such as Li Hongzhi (born 1951) began to teach it as a 'system of mind-body cultivation'. He founded the Falun Dafa (more popularly known as Falun Gong – 'the Wheel of Law') in 1992. In his teaching, the exercises allowed practitioners to get in touch with the energy of the universe, thus enabling them to access higher levels of existence.

Li describes five main exercises for practitioners to undertake. The Falun – Law Wheel – is situated in the lower abdomen, he claims, and by rotating it in line with the rotation of the universe, the practitioner dispenses with negative influences. This enables him or her to access cosmic energy, or *qi*. The philosophy of Falun Gong is based on *zhen-shan-ren* – truthfulness, compassion and forbearance – which is, of course, similar to the traditional precepts followed by Buddhists, followers of Confucianism and Daoists.

Some see Falun Gong as a new religion while other observers view it as the continuation of Chinese efforts to cultivate the mind and body. By 1999, there were estimated to be around 70 million practitioners of Falun Gong and the government began to view it as a threat. It started to receive negative coverage in state-run newspapers and practitioners protested at the state interference in religion. Following a demonstration by around 10,000 followers near government buildings in Beijing in April 1999, the Chinese leadership instigated a crackdown and a campaign of propaganda against the movement. In October 1999, Falun Gong was declared to be a 'heretical organisation' that was a risk to Chinese stability and it was made illegal. Hundreds of thousands of practitioners were imprisoned.

Li Hongzhi had fled to the United States three years previously but since then Falun Gong has continued to grow. In China, it is believed that millions still practise it illegally and there are hundreds of thousands more practitioners in around 70 countries around the world.

Vietnam

Following the political chaos that tore Vietnam apart in the twentieth century, four principal religious groups were left. These were Buddhism, Roman Catholicism, and two distinctly Vietnamese groups – Cao Dai and Hao Hao.

Cao Dai, which translates as 'Supreme Palace', is a syncretistic, monotheistic religion that was founded in the Southern Vietnamese city of Tay Ninh in 1926. Combining elements of Buddhism, Christianity, Daoism, Confucianism and Islam, its full name is Dai Dao Tam Ky Pho Do, which means 'great religion of the third period of revelation and salvation', also known as 'The Third Amnesty'. The first amnesty was with Buddha, founder of Buddhism, and Laozi, founder of Daoism. The second was with Moses and Jesus Christ. Cao Di is said to be the third and unsurpassable manifestation of God in the historical process of revelation.

The religion has its own leader – a pope-like figure – as well as priests, cardinals and bishops, as in the Catholic Church. In it, communication with God is received through trance and contact with the dead is especially important. Cao Di reveres a perplexing array of deceased well-known figures, including Victor Hugo, Sun Yat-sen, Joan of Arc and Louis Pasteur. Adherents are predominantly peasants who are attracted by its magical, spiritual aspects. They worship in temples and there are a great many rituals to be followed. Prayer, incense, meditation and exorcism are particularly important parts of worship, and women are permitted to become celebrants. The symbol of Cao Dai is the Divine Eye and it has around 5 million followers, primarily in Vietnam.

Hao Hao is a neo-Buddhist sect that was founded by Huynh Phu So (1920-47) in the village of Hao which is located near the Vietnamese border with Cambodia. In 1939, he was the victim of a sudden fit that seemed to cure him of all the other ailments he had been suffering from and turned him into a compelling preacher. He devised the new religion of Hao Hao, revising a number of Buddhist rituals and teaching that neither a holy man nor a holy place was required to be able to pray directly to God. The main tenets of his religion held that adherents should honour their parents, love their country, respect his version of Buddhism and love their fellow humans.

His secret was to communicate his message in such a way that it could be easily understood by peasants in teaching centres across Vietnam. The French colonial rulers of Vietnam detained him in a psychiatric hospital and then placed him under house arrest but it did not prevent him from continuing his work. He was eventually murdered in 1947 by the Vietnamese independence fighters, the Viet Minh, because he would not ally himself with them. Hao Hao remains a force to be reckoned with in southern Vietnam with around 2 million followers.

UFO and New Age Religions

A UFO religion can be defined as one in which the belief is that extraterrestrial beings travelling on unidentified flying objects are actually gods who come to earth and communicate with specific people. They become an element of belief of the faith system in question. The roots for these beliefs can be traced back to early science fiction or the category of literature known as weird fiction.

Probably the earliest example of this kind of belief was the Aetherius Society, founded by the Englishman, George King (1919-97), in 1955. King claimed to have had contact with aliens whom he described as 'Cosmic Masters' and it became the objective of followers to make further contact with these beings who would help humanity make a better future for itself. Despite King's passing in 1997, the Aetherius Society still exists, its membership international, but not large.

French-born Claude Vorilhon (born 1946) claims he founded Raëlism after an encounter with an extraterrestrial being in 1973. The alien explained to him that advanced beings, called Elohim, from another planet, created life on earth through the manipulation of DNA. They had sent 40 prophets to earth but humans had distorted their messages. Vorilhon, who now goes by the name of Raël, claims to have been given the mission of spreading this news and announcing that these extraterrestrials will return. In preparation for their return, he was ordered to build an embassy in a neutral country. He claims also at one point to have met and been taught by Jesus, Buddha, Moses and Muhammad.

The so-called Human Potential Movement (HPM) grew out of the 1960s counter-culture, based on the notion that we all have untapped potential within us. HPM aims to unleash that potential. Scientology could be said to fall between the categories of UFO religion and HPM. Founded by the science fiction author, L Ron Hubbard (1911-86) and based on his bestselling 1950 book, *Dianetics: The Modern Science of Mental Health*, it talks of extraterrestrial civilisations and past lives. It claims that we have all had many past lives, including lives in ancient advanced societies. It is traumatic memories from these lives that are the cause of mental and physical ailments. Scientology uses the process known as auditing to unleash the superhuman powers that adherents believe all humans possess. Hubbard wrote that a thetan – the scientology term for the soul – has a body and when it dies, the thetan goes to a landing site on Venus to be reprogrammed to forget previous existences. The thetan is then dumped back on earth and searches for a new body to inhabit. Other HPM groups could be said to include Erhard Seminar Training (est – now known as the Landmark Forum), the Silva Method, PSI Mind Development and the School of Economic Science, its teachings influenced by the Hindu philosophy Advaita Vedanta.

The New Age Movement (NAM) is as hard to define as HPM. NAM is an eclectic movement that believes that human nature is innately good and followers are disdainful of or disenchanted with organised religion. It is described variously as spiritual or Mind, Body, Spirit and is heavily influenced by the counter-culture of the 1960s, Theosophy, spiritualism and the occult influences of men such as the Swedish philosopher, Emanuel Swedenborg (1688-1772) and the German physician, Franz Mesmer (1734-1815). NAM flourished in Britain in the 1970s and then grew in the United States in the next two decades.

New Age is a very diverse religious category, but there are some identifiable themes, such as the spiritual authority of the self and a belief in non-human beings, with whom people can enter into dialogue, often using the process of channeling. Commonly, it is believed that humanity once lived in an age of spiritual wisdom and technological advancement but that it has degenerated into spiritual vacuity which will be remedied by the coming of the Age of Aquarius. New Age philosophy also incorporates healing, using alternative types of medicine and a desire to bring together spirituality and science.

Bibliography

The Religions Book, London: Dorling Kindersley, 2013

Bowker, John, *The Oxford Dictionary of World Religions*, Oxford: Oxford University Press, 1999

Bowker, John, *World Religions: The Great Faiths Explained*, London: Dorling Kindersley, 2006

Boyett, Jason, *12 Major Religions: The Beliefs, Rituals and Traditions of Humanity's Most Influential Faiths*, New York: Callisto, 2017

Hinnells, John R, *The Penguin Handbook of the World's Living Religions*, London: Penguin, 2010

O'Callaghan, Sean, *The Compact Guide to the World's Religions*, Oxford: Lion Hudson, 2010

Smart, Ninian, *The World's Religions*, Cambridge: Cambridge University Press, 1998

Smith, Huston, *The World's Religions*, San Francisco: HarperOne, 2009

Index

13 Principles of Faith, 165
39 Articles, 191

'Abdu'l-Bahá, 222-4
AC Bhaktivedanta Prabhupada, 238
Abraham (also Abram/Ibrahim),
    158, 159, 164, 204, 213, 215
Adi Granth Sahib, 129, 133
Aetherius Society, 245
Afghanistan, 88, 207, 211
Africa, 201, 202, 207, 208, 217, 221,
    227, 234
afterlife, 20, 22, 28, 29, 46, 50, 60
agnosticism, 225-6
ahimsa, 90, 96, 124
Ahura Mazda, 31, 33
alien being (also extraterrestrial), 13,
    244-5
Allah, 101, 205, 206, 213, 214, 216,
    217
al-Qaeda, 210
Amaterasu, 149, 150
Ameretat, 33
America, 18, 21, 68, 71, 90, 196,
    202, 203, 220, 221, 237, 239
ancestor worship/cult, 76, 141, 151,
    152, 230, 231
Anglican Church, 191, 194, 202,
    226
Angra Mainyu, 31, 33
animist, 148, 227
Aphrodite, 43-4, 49, 62, 236

Apollo, 43, 62
Apostle (also Disciple), 178, 179,
    180, 181, 182, 200
Arabia, 129, 184, 204, 205
Aranyakas, 84, 94
Archangel Gabriel (Jebreel), 205,
    217
Ares, 41, 43, 44, 62
arihant, 105, 107, 109, 119, 126
Arius, 182, 183
Armageddon, 197
Armaiti, 33
Arsuf, Battle of, 187
Artemis, 41, 43
asceticism (ascetic), 85, 104, 113,
    121, 122, 126, 182, 216
Asclepius, 45, 52
Asha, 31, 33
atheism, 194, 224-5, 226
Athena, 41-2
Augustine of Canterbury, 56, 184
Augustus, Emperor, 24, 50, 51, 177
Austria, 18, 163, 187
Avesta, 31, 36
Ayatollah Khomeini, 210
Aztecs, 68, 69, 72, 73-4

Báb, the, 220
Baghdad, 37, 208, 220
Baha'í Faith, 220-4
Bahá'u'lláh Mirza Husayn 'Ali
    Nuri, 220, 221, 223, 224

Bangladesh, 81, 108
baptism, 135, 136, 178, 189, 195, 196, 201
Baptist Church, 195, 196
ben Maimon, Moses (Maimonides/Rambam), 165-6
Berg, David, 'The Last Endtime Prophet', 236
Bhagavad Gita, 92, 95
Bhagwan Shree Rajneesh, 238
bhakti, 82, 93
Bhakti movement/yoga, 87, 92
Bible, the, 158, 161, 163, 164, 169, 170, 171, 175, 196, 224, 227
bodhisattva, 109, 111, 114, 118, 119
Book of Mormon, 196
Book of Songs, 140, 141
Book of the Dead, The, 28, 29
Bosnia, 211
Brahma(n), 82, 85, 91, 93, 94, 97, 105
Brahmanism, 84, 86, 89
Brahmin, 84, 88, 94, 98, 102, 113
Brazil, 2, 230
Bronze Age, 39, 40, 41, 58
Buddhism, 13, 82, 86, 96, 101-18, 119, 125, 144, 148, 149, 150, 225, 239-41, 243, 244
Buddhist Council (First, Second, Third, Fourth), 106-8, 116-7
burial, 11, 16, 17, 18, 21, 63, 83, 140

Calvin, John, 190
Calvinism, 190, 192, 195
Canada, 120, 127, 234
Candomblé, 230-1
Cao Dai (Dai Dao Tam Ky Pho Do), 243
Caribbean, 228, 229, 230
Catholic, 190, 191, 192, 193, 194, 229, 230, 243
Catholicism, 81, 100, 185, 188, 190, 191, 192, 194, 195, 200, 202,

celibacy, 70, 124, 189
Central America, 68, 69, 76
Chechnya, 211
Children of God, 236
China, 64, 108, 109, 110, 118, 138-46, 148, 202, 208, 241-2
Christian Science, 235
Christianity, 13, 33, 52, 53, 54, 56, 60, 61, 66, 80, 88, 89, 150, 162, 170, 173, 176-203, 213, 226, 230, 234, 235, 237, 243
Christmas, 197
Church of England, 191, 194, 203
Church of Jesus Christ of Latter-Day
Saints (Mormon Church), 196-7
circumcision, 162, 166
Civetot, Battle of, 186
commandments, 158, 160, 161, 163, 164, 165, 166, 169
Communist, 193, 221, 241
Confucianism, 13, 101, 138, 139-40, 144, 148, 149, 242, 243
Confucius, 138, 139, 140, 141, 142, 143, 144, 241
Congregationalism, 195
Constantine, Emperor, 52, 182, 183, 199
Constantinople, 184, 185, 188, 207
Council of Nicaea, First, 182-3
Council, 108, 116, 117
Council of Trent, 191-2
Counter-Reformation, 191-2
Covenant, 163-4
Cronus, 41, 42, 43, 44
crucifixion, 176, 180, 198, 200
Crusade, 162, 186, 187, 188
Cuba, 228, 229
cult, 20, 45, 46, 50, 52, 58, 74, 76, 86, 114, 152, 203, 234

Dagda, 54
Dalai Lama, 110, 240
dao, 145, 146
Daode jing, 144, 145, 146
Daoism, 13, 101, 144, 146, 241, 243
Darwin, Charles, 226
Day of Judgement (Judgement Day), 177, 196, 213
de Loyola, Ignatius, 192
Demeter, 41, 42
Deva, 86
dharma, 84, 89, 102, 105, 106, 112, 115, 116, 117, 222, 240
Dhimmis, 37, 87
Digambara Jainism, 120, 121, 122, 123
Dionysus, 41, 44, 46
disciple, 89, 105, 106, 107, 114, 121, 122, 127, 140, 200
Druidism, 54, 55, 56, 227
DT Suzuki, 239
dukkha, 84, 110, 240

Easter, 56, 197
Eddy, Mary Baker, 235
Edict of Milan, 52
Egypt, 22, 24-9, 50, 159, 160, 162, 167, 168, 169, 185, 207, 209, 210
Eightfold Path, 104, 110, 111, 112, 115
Elizabeth I, Queen, 190
Engaged Buddhism, 240, 241
England, 22, 56, 163, 187, 190, 191, 194, 195, 203, 240
enlightenment, 96, 102, 104, 105, 106, 110, 113, 114, 115, 119, 125
Eros, 45
Eucharist, 189, 192, 195, 200
excommunication, 183, 190
Exodus, 160, 167, 168, 169

Falun Gong (formerly Falun Dafa), 241, 242
Family International, The, 236
fasting, 70, 99, 125, 168, 170, 214, 215
fertility, 18, 19, 20, 25, 42, 50, 53, 54, 59, 66, 70, 83
Feuerbach, Ludwig, 193
figurines, 18, 20, 25, 39, 40, 82
Five Pillars of Islam, 214
France, 18, 19, 163, 187, 190, 191, 193, 207
French Revolution, 193, 225
Freud, Sigmund, 193

Galilee, 173, 177, 178, 179
Gandhi, Mohandas, 90
Gathas, 30, 31, 32, 36
Germany, 65, 163, 189, 192, 202
Gobind Singh, 132, 133, 135
Goddess Spirituality, 227
Golden Temple, 131, 132
Gospels, 177, 178, 198, 199, 213
Greece, 34, 35, 39-47, 46, 48, 49, 53, 55, 62, 162, 176, 185, 200, 208, 224
Gregory the Great, Pope, 56, 184
Guru Amar Das, 131
Guru Angad, 130, 131
Guru Arjan, 131, 132
Guru Granth Sahib, 128, 134, 135
Guru Hargobind, 132
Guru Nanak, 127-9, 130, 135
Guru Ram Das, 131

Hades, 41, 45
Hadith, 208, 214
Hajj, 215
Hao Hao, 243, 244
Hare Krishna movement (International Society for

Krishna Consciousness), 90, 92, 238

Hattin, Battle of, 187

Haurvatat, 33

Heathenism, 227

heaven, 11, 32, 39, 71, 91, 112, 113, 139, 143, 176, 178, 180, 196, 197, 198, 199, 200

Heaven, 66, 139, 141, 143, 186, 199, 234

Hebe, 45

Hebrew, 161, 166, 168, 169, 170, 171, 172, 176

hell, 32, 33, 34, 121, 196

Henry VIII, King, 190, 191, 194

Hephaestus, 44

Hera, 41, 42, 43, 44

Heracles, 45, 62

Hermes, 41, 44

Hestia, 41, 44, 46, 62

Hinduism, 9, 13, 80-100, 122, 123, 128, 129, 130, 132, 133, 134, 202, 208, 225, 237-9, 246

Holland, 192

Holocaust, 163, 174

Holy Communion, 185, 195, 200

Holy Land, 181, 185, 187, 188

Holy Spirit, 178, 183, 185, 197, 237

House of Justice Universal, 221, 222, 224

Hubbard, L Ron, 245, 246

Human Potential Movement (HPM), 245-6

Hus, Jan, 189

Huynh Phu So, 244

imam, 212, 213

immortality, 33, 80, 146, 197

Incas, 75-7

India, 34, 36, 38, 66, 79-136, 202, 208, 209, 210, 217, 221, 237, 238, 239

Indonesia, 18, 81, 208

indulgences, 188, 189

International Society for Krishna Consciousness, 92, 238

Iran, 30, 34, 37, 38, 62, 65, 66, 100, 209, 210, 213, 220, 221

Iraq, 159, 207, 211

Ireland, 53, 56, 184, 191

Isaac, 158, 159

Ishmael, 159, 215

Islam, 13, 36, 37, 80, 86, 87, 88, 108, 123, 128, 129, 132, 133, 162, 163, 184, 185, 186, 187, 194, 198, 204-18, 221, 243

Islamic Revolution (Iran), 210

Islamic State, 210

Israel, 158, 159, 160, 161, 163, 164, 167, 174, 175, 220, 221

Jacob, 158, 159, 160

Jah, 227, 228

Jainism, 82, 88, 96, 102, 119-26, 225

Jamaica, 227

Japan, 109, 118, 147-55, 240

Jehovah's Witnesses, 197

Jerusalem, 161, 163, 170, 172, 180, 184, 186, 187

Jesuits, Society of, 192

Jesus Christ, 36, 55, 81, 101, 102, 162, 176-80, 181, 182, 183, 195, 196, 197, 198, 199, 200, 201, 203, 213, 227, 235, 236, 243, 245

John the Baptist, 178, 179, 201

Jordan, 159

Judaism, 13, 158-75, 181, 198, 204, 207, 213

Judea, 171, 177, 178

Jupiter, 49, 52

Kabbalah, 172-3

kami, 12, 147, 148, 149, 151, 153, 154
Kaplan, Mordecai, 175
karma, 82, 84, 96, 125
Kelsang Gyatso, 240
Kevala Jnana, 121, 122, 123
Khalsa, 128, 132, 135
King, George, 245
Kitab-i-Aqdas (The Most Holy Book), 223
Kitab-i-Iqan (The Book of Certitude), 224
Knox, John, 190
Kojiki, 154
Korea, 109, 118, 202, 236, 237
Krishna, 87, 90, 92, 93, 95
Kshathra, 33

Laozi, 144-6, 243
Last Supper, 180, 198, 200
Latin, 49, 100, 185, 188, 189, 203, 221
Lebanon, 159
Li Hongzhi, 241, 242
Libya, 207
life after death, 17, 18, 19
Love Family, 235-6
Luther, Martin, 189
Lutheranism, 189, 190, 192, 194, 195, 202

Mahabharata, 94, 95
Maharishi Mahesh Yogi, 238
Mahayana Buddhism, 109, 111, 117, 118
Malaysia, 81, 208
Mandate of Heaven, 139, 141, 143
mantra, 98, 126, 238, 240
Marx, Karl, 193
Mary, Queen, 190
Maududi, Abul A'la, 210
Mauritius, 81

Maya, 70-1
Mecca, 205, 206, 209, 215
meditation, 94, 96, 104, 105, 109, 111, 113, 115, 125, 135, 146, 216, 238, 240, 241, 243
Meiji Restoration, 150-1
Mesmer , Franz, 246
Messiah, the, 166, 176, 177, 180, 197
Methodism, 195
Mexico, 68, 69, 70, 71, 72, 73, 203, 228
Middle East, 22, 158, 163, 210
Milan, Edict of, 52, 182
Miller, William, 196, 234
Mishnah, 166, 171-2
missionary, 56, 57, 82, 89, 150, 184, 195, 197, 201, 209, 221, 240
moksha, 84, 85, 96, 124, 126
Mongols, 63-4
monotheism, 97, 127, 158, 160, 164, 198, 213, 243
monuments, 21-22
Moon, Sun Myung, 236, 237
Moses, 160, 161, 165, 168, 169, 170, 213, 243, 245
Muhammad, Prophet the, 37, 101, 204-6, 207, 208, 211, 212, 213, 214, 216, 217, 218, 245
Mühlberg, Battle of, 190
mysticism, 152, 172, 173, 224

Naam Japna, 130, 135
Neolithic period, 16, 20, 21
Nepal, 81, 100, 103, 105
New Age, 220, 244, 246, 247
New Age Movement (NAM), 246
New Kadampa Tradition, 240
New Testament, 177, 181
Nicene Creed, 183, 184, 197
Nichiren Buddhism, 240
Nigeria, 202

Ninety-Five Theses, 189

nirvana, 106, 109, 110, 111, 115

Odin (Wodin), 58, 59, 60

offerings, 16, 20, 26, 27, 40, 45, 51, 63, 64, 68, 69, 71, 75, 76, 98, 99, 115, 153

Old Testament, 162, 170, 176, 197

Olmecs, 69-70

Olodumare, 229, 231

Olympian (Mount Olympus), 41, 44, 45

Orthodox Judaism, 166, 168, 174, 175

Osiris, 28, 29, 50

paganism, 54, 56, 65, 66, 197, 226

Pakistan, 81, 88, 90, 129, 207

Paleolithic period, 16, 17, 18, 19

Palestinian territories, 159

Pali Canon, 107, 108, 116-7

Paramahansa Yogananda, 237

Passover, 168, 180

Patriarchs, 159, 160

Patrick, St, 56, 184

Paul III, Pope, 191

Peace of Augsburg, 190

Pentecostal Church, 201, 202

Persephone, 42, 45

Persia, 13, 31, 34, 35, 36, 37, 38, 50, 62, 66, 80, 207, 220

Peru, 68, 74, 75

Philippines, The, 81, 202, 208

pilgrimage, 27, 96, 99, 114, 130, 185, 206, 209, 215, 238

polytheism, 68, 97, 159

Poseidon, 41, 42

prayer, 12, 28, 51, 56, 80, 98, 126, 153, 154, 165, 167, 168, 171, 179, 192, 200, 214, 215, 222, 235, 238, 243

Presbyterianism, 190, 195

Protestantism, 190, 191, 192, 194, 196, 202

Psalms, 213

puja, 98, 99, 115

Punjab, 88, 127, 128, 129, 130, 133

Purana, Devi-Bhagavata, 93

Puranas, 85, 87, 89, 92

purification, 96, 99, 153, 154, 179, 215, 216

pyramid, 24, 69, 71, 72

Qigong, 241

Quetzalcoatl, 69, 71, 72

Qur'an, 204, 206, 208, 210, 211, 212, 213, 214, 215, 217-8, 224

Qutb, Sayyid, 210

Raëlism, 245

Ragnarok, 60-1

Rahula, 103, 106

Rajneesh movement, 238-9

Ramadan, 214, 218

Ramakrishna, 89, 237

Ramayana, 95, 120

Rastafarianism, 227-8

rebirth, 74, 85, 96, 98, 109, 110, 115, 119, 121, 123, 124

Reformation, 188-91, 192, 196, 203

reincarnation, 84, 110, 134

relics, 106, 113, 114

ren, 141, 143, 242

Rhea, 41, 42, 44

Richard I, 'the Lionheart', 187

rightly guided caliphs, 212, 217

Rightly Guided Caliphs, 212, 217

Rikkokushi, 154

Roman Catholicism, 77, 165, 192, 203, 229, 243

Roman Empire, 13, 24, 36, 39, 48-52, 53, 56, 162, 177, 180, 181, 182, 183, 184, 185, 187, 191

Rowe, William L, 225

Sabbath (see also *Shabatt*), 163, 169, 171, 179, 196, 199
sacrifice, animal, 40, 45, 55, 63, 65, 70, 84, 159, 229
    general, 22, 25, 45, 49, 60, 64, 65, 75, 76, 82, 83, 84, 94, 99, 139, 161, 163, 172, 200, 229
    human, 40, 55, 63, 65, 70-1, 72, 73-4, 76, 159, 197
Salat, 214
samsara, 84, 96, 106, 109, 110, 119
sangha, 105, 106, 107, 115
Sanskrit, 80, 82, 83, 85, 86, 98, 99, 100, 117, 118, 119, 134
Santeria, 228-9, 231
Sathya Sai Organisation, 238
Scandinavia, 34, 58, 59, 65, 192, 194
science, 12, 42, 85, 193, 208, 209, 222, 223, 225, 245, 247
Scientology, 245, 246
Scotland, 53, 190, 192
Scythians, 62-3
Second Coming, 177, 196, 197, 198, 227, 234
Selassie, Haile, Emperor of Ethiopia 227, 228
Self-Realization Fellowship, 237
Seventh-day Adventist Church, 196, 234
Shabbat (see also Sabbath), 166, 167, 168, 169
Shahada, 214
Shaivism, 91
Shaktism, 86, 93
Shang, 138-9
Shari'a, 208, 212
Shi'a Muslims, 211-3, 214
Shinto, 12, 147-8, 149, 150, 151-5
Shiva, 80, 82, 83, 86, 91, 93
Shvetambara Jainism, 120, 121, 122, 123, 124

Siddhartha Gautama (Gautama Buddha), 103, 104, 121, 122
Sikhism, 13, 88, 127-36
Slavs, 65-6,
Soka Gakkai International (SGI), 240
Son of God, 176, 180, 197
South America, 68, 201
Southeast Asia, 21, 108, 114, 221
Spain, 19, 68, 73, 77, 173, 208, 228
Spring and Autumn Annals, 140
Sramana, 102, 103
Sri Lanka, 81, 107, 108, 116
state religion, 52, 70, 76, 87, 88, 144, 149, 150, 151, 152, 182
Sufism, 215-7
Sunni Muslims, 88, 211-3, 214
surah, 210, 211, 217
Surah, 210, 211, 217
Sutra, 109, 117, 118, 121, 125, 240
Sutta, 101, 104, 116
Swedenborg, Emanuel, 246
Switzerland, 192, 234
Syria, 187, 207

tai chi, 146
Talmud, 171, 172, 175
Tanakh (*Mikra*/Hebrew Bible), 170-1
Ten Commandments, 160
Theravada Buddhism, 107, 108, 109, 111, 116, 240
Thirty Years' War, 191
Thor, 59, 60, 65
Three Pillars of Sikhism, 135
Tibet, 107, 108, 109, 110, 114, 129, 240
Tirthankaras, 102, 119-20, 125, 126
Titans, 41, 43
Toltecs, 71-2
Torah, 160, 162, 163, 165, 166, 167, 168-70, 171, 213

Tours, Battle of, 207
Transcendental Meditation, 90, 238
transubstantiation, 195, 200
Trinity, the, 196, 197
Tuatha, 53, 54
Twelve Tribes of Israel, 160

UFO religion, 244-5
underworld, 29, 45, 46, 47, 54, 66, 71, 74
Unification Church, 236, 237
United Kingdom, 81, 120, 127, 234
United States, 81, 120, 127, 173, 174, 175, 194, 195, 196, 229, 234, 235, 237, 239, 242, 246
Upanishads, 84, 87, 91, 92, 94, 95
Urban, Pope, 185, 186
USSR, 194

Vaishnavism, 85, 92
Vardhamana Mahavira, 102, 119, 120-4
Vajrayana Buddhism, 109, 110
Vatican, 81, 188, 221
Vedanta, 237, 246
Vedas, 13, 81, 83, 93, 94, 95
Vedic religion, 13, 66, 81, 83, 84, 89, 91, 94, 99, 100, 102
Venus, 18, 49, 246
Vietnam, 243-4
Vipassana movment, 240
Vishnu, 85, 86, 91, 92, 93
Vivekananda, 90, 237
Vohu Manah, 30, 33
Vorilhon, Claude, 245

Wesley, John, 195
Wicca, 227
wu wei, 145, 146
Wycliffe, John, 189

Yasna, 32, 36
yin and *yang*, 139, 146
Yin and *Yang*, 139, 146
yoga, 82, 85, 92, 104, 237, 238
Yogoda Satsanga Society of India, 237
Yoruba, 229, 230

Zakat, 215
Zen Buddhism, 109, 239, 241
Zeus, 39, 41-2, 43, 44, 49, 62, 101
Zoroaster (Zarathustra), 30-36
Zoroastrianism, 13, 30-38, 88